# Saltwater Intrusion in the Surficial Aquifer System of the Big Cypress Basin, Southwest Florida, and a Proposed Plan for Improved Salinity Monitoring

By Scott T. Prinos

Prepared in cooperation with the South Florida Water Management District

Open-File Report 2013–1088

U.S. Department of the Interior
U.S. Geological Survey

**U.S. Department of the Interior**
SALLY JEWELL, Secretary

**U.S. Geological Survey**
Suzette M. Kimball, Acting Director

U.S. Geological Survey, Reston, Virginia: 2013

For more information on the USGS—the Federal source for science about the Earth, its natural and living resources, natural hazards, and the environment, visit http://www.usgs.gov or call 1–888–ASK–USGS.

For an overview of USGS information products, including maps, imagery, and publications, visit http://www.usgs.gov/pubprod

To order this and other USGS information products, visit http://store.usgs.gov

Suggested citation:
Prinos, S.T., 2013, Saltwater intrusion in the surficial aquifer system of the Big Cypress Basin, southwest Florida, and a proposed plan for improved salinity monitoring: U.S. Geological Survey Open-File Report 2013–1088, 58 p., *http://pubs.usgs.gov/of/2013/1088/*.

# Contents

# Figures

## Tables

# Appendixes

[Appendix files are available online at *http://pubs.usgs.gov/of/2013/1088/*]

# Conversion Factors

Inch/Pound to SI

| Multiply | By | To obtain |
|---|---|---|
| **Length** | | |
| inch (in.) | 2.54 | centimeter (cm) |
| inch (in.) | 25.4 | millimeter (mm) |
| foot (ft) | 0.3048 | meter (m) |
| mile (mi) | 1.609 | kilometer (km) |
| **Area** | | |
| square inch (in$^2$) | 6.452 | square centimeter (cm$^2$) |
| square mile (mi$^2$) | 259.0 | hectare (ha) |
| square mile (mi$^2$) | 2.590 | square kilometer (km$^2$) |
| **Volume** | | |
| gallon (gal) | 3.785 | liter (L) |
| gallon (gal) | 0.003785 | cubic meter (m$^3$) |
| gallon (gal) | 3.785 | cubic decimeter (dm$^3$) |
| million gallons (Mgal) | 3,785 | cubic meter (m$^3$) |
| **Flow rate** | | |
| gallon per minute (gal/min) | 0.06309 | liter per second (L/s) |
| million gallons per day (Mgal/d) | 0.04381 | cubic meter per second (m$^3$/s) |
| million gallons per month (Mgal/mo) | 3,785 | cubic meter per month (m$^3$/mo) |

Vertical coordinate information is referenced to the National Geodetic Vertical Datum of 1929 (NGVD 29).

Horizontal coordinate information is referenced to the North American Datum of 1983 (NAD 83).

Altitude, as used in this report, refers to distance above the vertical datum.

*Transmissivity: The standard unit for transmissivity is cubic foot per day per square foot times foot of aquifer thickness [(ft3/d)/ft2]ft. In this report, the mathematically reduced form, foot squared per day (ft2/d), is used for convenience.

Specific conductance is given in microsiemens per centimeter at 25 degrees Celsius (µS/cm at 25 °C).

Concentrations of chemical constituents in water are given either in milligrams per liter (mg/L) or micrograms per liter (µg/L).

# Abbreviations

| | |
|---|---|
| bls | below land surface |
| BOG | Bureau of Oil and Gas |
| CCPCPD | Collier County Pollution Control and Prevention Department |
| CRP | continuous resistivity profiling |
| DC | direct current |
| FDEP | Florida Department of Environmental Protection |
| FGS | Florida Geological Survey |

| | |
|---|---|
| FLUWID | Florida unique well identification |
| GIS | geographic information system |
| GPS | Global Positioning System |
| HEM | Helicopter Electromagnetic |
| JSWIM | Joint Saltwater Intrusion Monitoring |
| LCNRD | Lee County Natural Resources Division |
| NWIS | National Water Information System |
| NE1 | Phase 1 Examination of Existing Salinity Monitoring in Southwest Florida |
| ppt | parts per thousand |
| PSU | practical salinity unit |
| PVC | polyvinyl chloride |
| QA/QC | quality assurance/quality control |
| RSM | Regional Simulation Model |
| SFWMD | South Florida Water Management District |
| SFWMD-SWIMM | South Florida Water Management District Saltwater Intrusion Monitoring and Management |
| SOP | standard operating procedure |
| STORET | Data Storage and Retrieval System |
| TEM | Time-Domain Electromagnetic |
| TSEMIL | Time-Series Electromagnetic Induction Log |
| USGS | U.S. Geological Survey |
| USEPA | U.S. Environmental Protection Agency |
| USGS-COOP-SWIM | U.S. Geological Survey Cooperative Saltwater Intrusion Monitoring |
| WILMA | Well Inventory and Lithological Geophysical Maintenance Application |
| WRS | Water Resources Solutions Inc. |

# Saltwater Intrusion in the Surficial Aquifer System of the Big Cypress Basin, Southwest Florida, and a Plan for Improved Salinity Monitoring

By Scott T. Prinos

## Abstract

The installation of drainage canals, poorly cased wells, and water-supply withdrawals have led to saltwater intrusion in the primary water-use aquifers in southwest Florida. Increasing population and water use have exacerbated this problem. Installation of water-control structures, well-plugging projects, and regulation of water use have slowed saltwater intrusion, but the chloride concentration of samples from some of the monitoring wells in this area indicates that saltwater intrusion continues to occur. In addition, rising sea level could increase the rate and extent of saltwater intrusion.

The existing saltwater intrusion monitoring network was examined and found to lack the necessary organization, spatial distribution, and design to properly evaluate saltwater intrusion. The most recent hydrogeologic framework of southwest Florida indicates that some wells may be open to multiple aquifers or have an incorrect aquifer designation. Some of the sampling methods being used could result in poor-quality data. Some older wells are badly corroded, obstructed, or damaged and may not yield useable samples. Saltwater in some of the canals is in close proximity to coastal well fields. In some instances, saltwater occasionally occurs upstream from coastal salinity control structures.

These factors lead to an incomplete understanding of the extent and threat of saltwater intrusion in southwest Florida. A proposed plan to improve the saltwater intrusion monitoring network in the South Florida Water Management District's Big Cypress Basin describes improvements in (1) network management, (2) quality assurance, (3) documentation, (4) training, and (5) data accessibility. The plan describes improvements to hydrostratigraphic and geospatial network coverage that can be accomplished using additional monitoring, surface geophysical surveys, and borehole geophysical logging. Sampling methods and improvements to monitoring well design are described in detail. Geochemical analyses that provide insights concerning the sources of saltwater in the aquifers are described. The requirement to abandon inactive wells is discussed.

## Introduction

In the early to mid-20th century, saltwater began to intrude the aquifers of southwest Florida (fig. 1) because of (1) lateral encroachment from the Gulf of Mexico caused by over drainage and water supply withdrawals; (2) infiltration from tidal marshes, estuaries, and bays; (3) direct leakage of saltwater from canals; (4) movement of residual or connate saltwater; and (5) upward or downward leakage through poorly cased boreholes or leaky semiconfining units. This saltwater eventually contaminated the first well field of the city of Naples located between Naples Bay and the Gulf of Mexico. Water with concentrations of sodium greater than 160 milligrams per liter (mg/L) or chloride greater than 250 mg/L exceeds drinking water standards (Florida Department of Health, 2005; U.S. Environmental Protection Agency, 2011a, b).

Saltwater intrusion in southwest Florida remains a concern because population has continued to increase and water use has generally also increased, except for recent years, when water restrictions have been in place (fig. 2). These changes can potentially affect the extent and magnitude of saltwater intrusion in coastal aquifers in this area. During 1970 to 2008, estimated population in Collier County (fig. 1), for example, increased from 38,040 to 321,520 (U.S. Census Bureau, 2011) and water use in the county increased from 5.0 to 80.6 million gallons per day (Mgal/d; fig. 2; Marella, 2009; Richard Marella U.S. Geological Survey, written commun., August 25, 2011). The surficial aquifer system, including the lower Tamiami and water-table aquifers, provided about 46 percent of the water used in Collier County in 2005 (Marella, 2009). Some of the public water supply well fields that provide water from the surficial aquifer system are close to the Gulf of Mexico (fig. 1) and may be particularly vulnerable to contamination by encroaching saltwater. The city of Naples Coastal Ridge well field (fig. 1), for example, in which wells are completed in the lower Tamiami aquifer, is within 1.5 miles (mi) of the Gulf. Evidence of saltwater intrusion during this period is seen in monitoring wells open to the water-table and lower Tamiami aquifers (fig. 3).

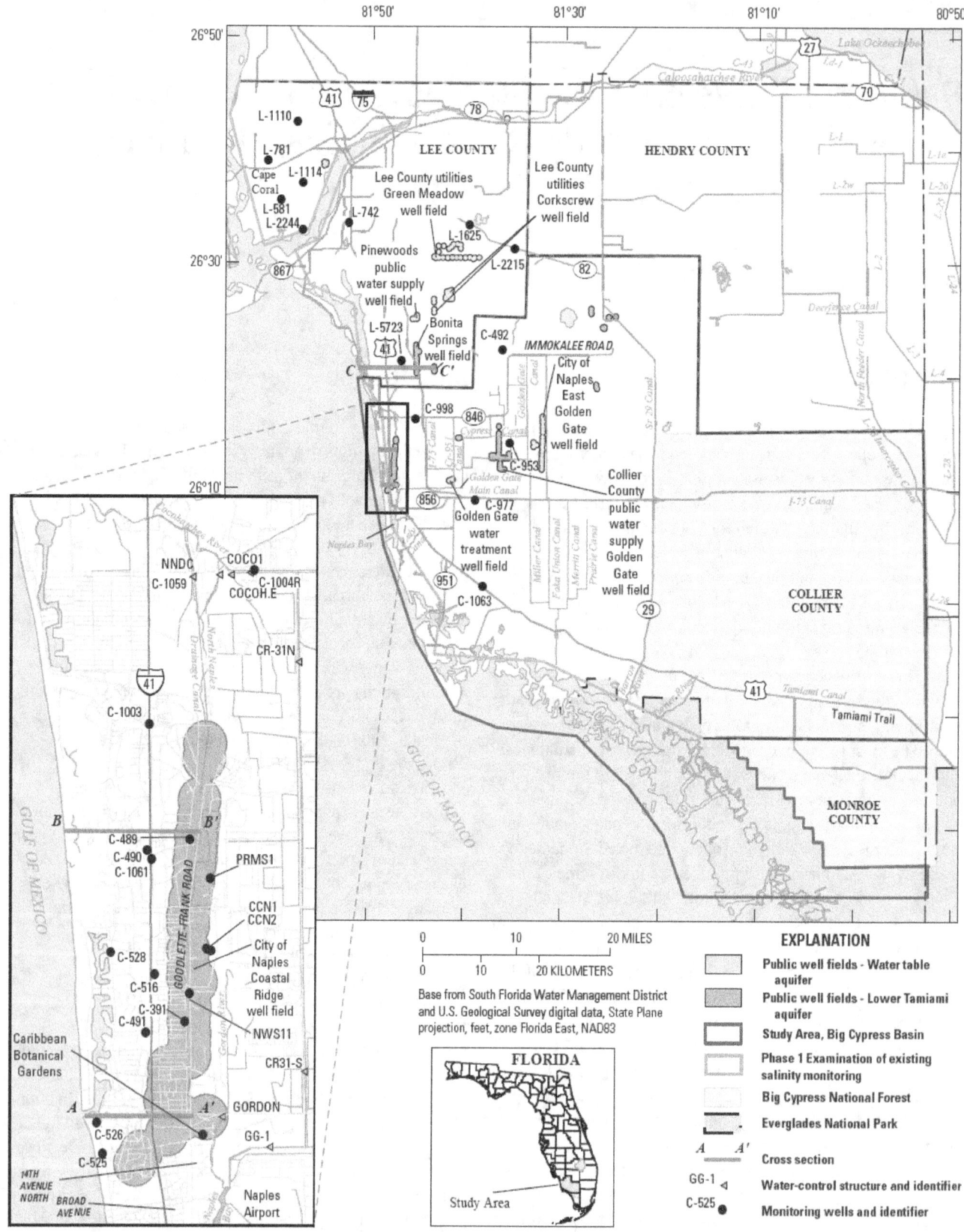

**Figure 1.**    Location of the Big Cypress Basin, which is the study area for this project, the area of the Phase 1 Examination of Existing Salinity Monitoring, public water-supply well fields, and cross sections. CCN1 and CCN2 are wells 1 and 2 of the County Club of Naples. NWS11 is Naples water supply well 11. PRMS1 is Pine Ridge Middle School well 1.

Salinity information is collected through the South Florida Water Management District Saltwater Intrusion Monitoring and Management (SFWMD-SWIMM) network, the U.S. Geological Survey Cooperative Saltwater Intrusion Monitoring (USGS-COOP-SWIM) network, and monitoring networks operated by the city of Cape Coral, Collier County Pollution Control and Prevention Department (CCPCPD), and Lee County Natural Resources Division (LCNRD). Each organization has different goals in collecting this information, but the combined network could be considered to be a joint saltwater intrusion monitoring (JSWIM) network. Most of the information from this JSWIM network has been entered into local, State, or Federal databases and is used by water managers to guide their decisions as they work to preserve fresh groundwater resources in southwest Florida, including the Big Cypress Basin.

If the information required by managers for evaluating saltwater intrusion is not provided, public water supply well fields may unexpectedly become contaminated. If saltwater intrudes into the well fields, it may take decades before the affected water once again becomes potable. The JSWIM network, therefore, was the focus of a previously unpublished SFWMD and USGS cooperative geospatial assessment

entitled "Phase 1 Examination of Existing Salinity Monitoring in Southwest Florida" (henceforth called the NE1, which stands for network examination 1). This examination evaluated the JSWIM network in the water-table, lower Tamiami, sandstone, and mid-Hawthorn aquifers in Lee and Collier Counties (fig. 1). The intent of the NE1 was to determine if any additional issues should be addressed by a more extensive hydrologic study. The NE1, completed on October 3, 2008, identified a number of deficiencies in monitoring that limited the ability of water managers to accurately evaluate saltwater intrusion. The preliminary findings were presented in a meeting at the completion of phase 1 so that decisions concerning additional phases could be considered. The USGS, in cooperation with the SFWMD, conducted a study to formally document the findings of the NE1 and to develop a network improvement strategy that would address the deficiencies in the existing monitoring network in the surficial aquifer system within the Big Cypress Basin (fig. 1).

Throughout this report, "salinity" is a general term used to describe the concentration of dissolved solids or chloride concentration of water samples, which may be directly measured by electrical conductivity of water, determined by chemical analysis of water samples, or indirectly detected

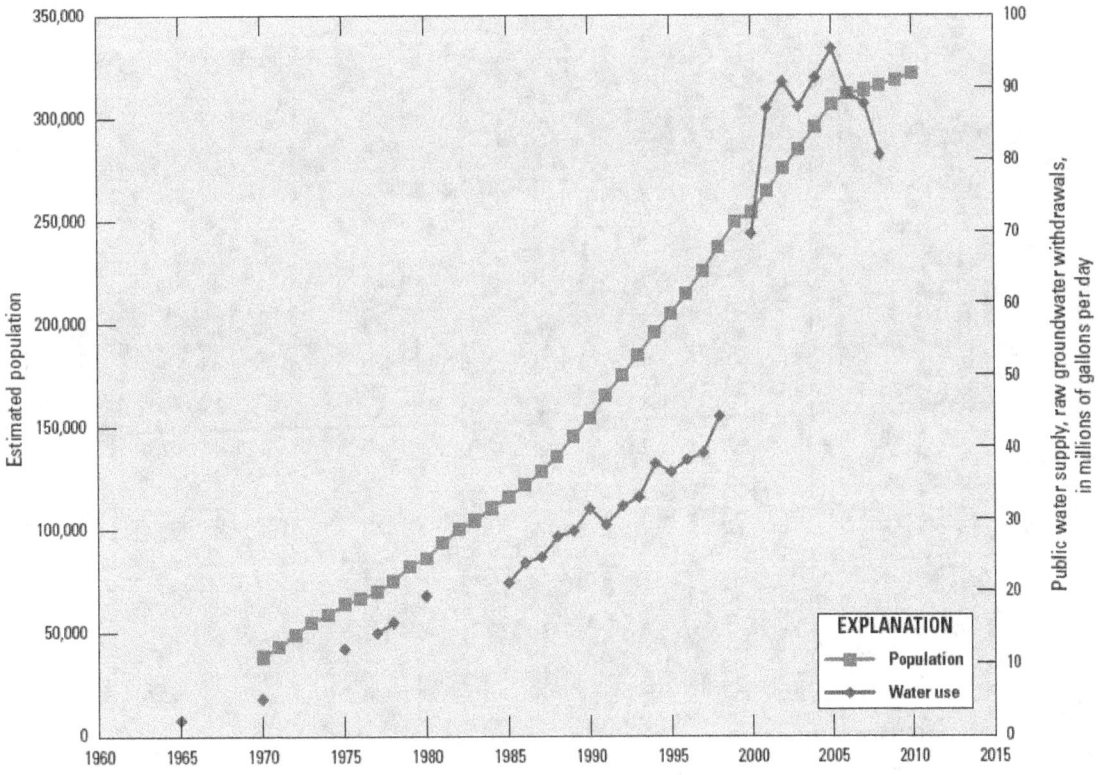

**Figure 2.**    Population and groundwater use in Collier County. Based on data from the U.S. Census Bureau (2011), Marella (2009), and Richard Marella (U.S. Geological Survey, written commun., August 25, 2011).

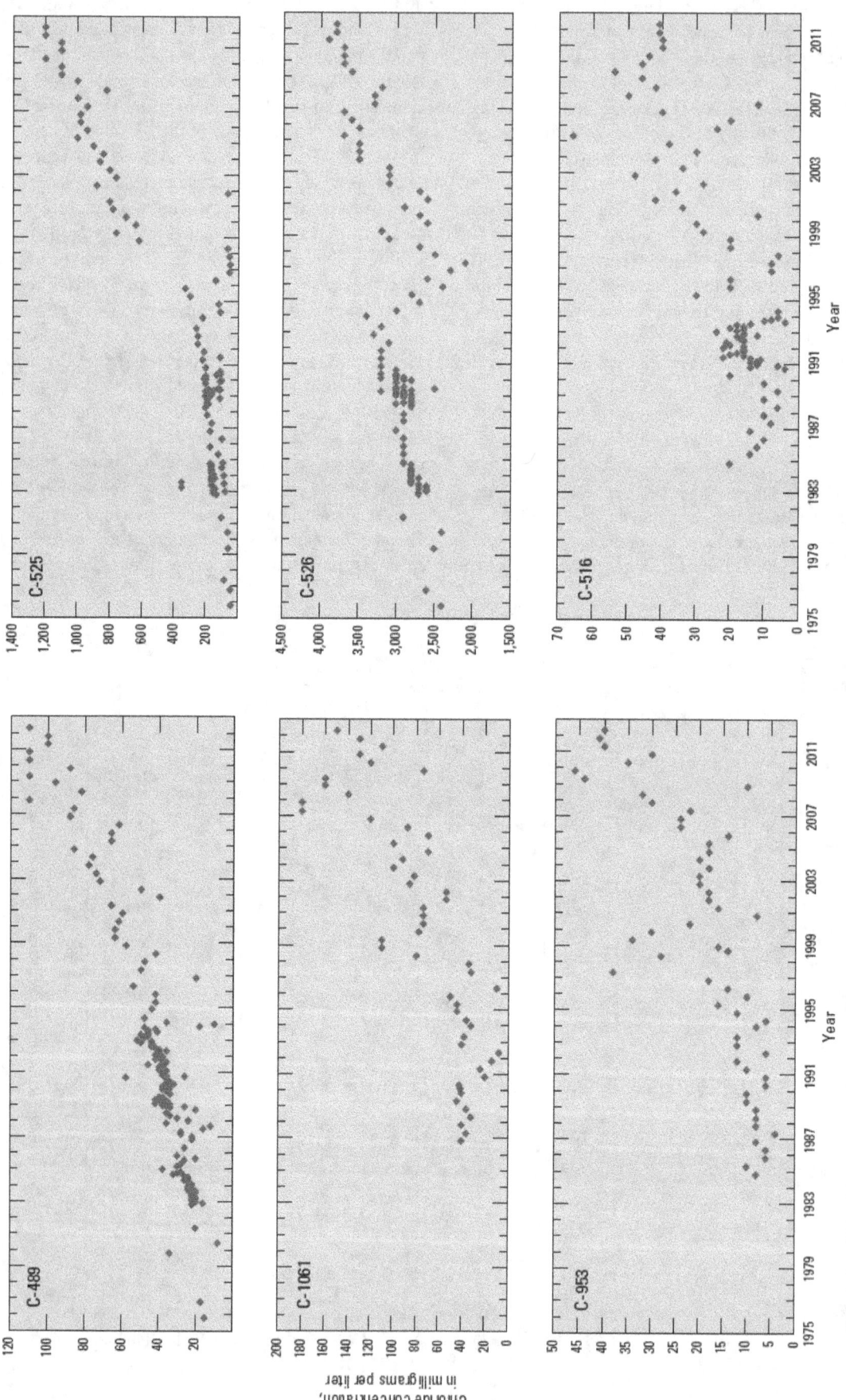

**Figure 3.**    Chloride concentration of water samples collected from monitoring wells C-489, C-516, C-525, and C-526 completed in the lower Tamiami aquifer and monitoring wells C-953 and C-1061 completed in the water-table aquifer.

by geophysical measurements of bulk resistivity/conductivity. In some instances, salinity is expressed either in practical salinity units (PSU) or in parts per thousand (ppt). The term "saltwater intrusion" refers to saltwater that has entered previously fresh portions of the aquifer regardless of the sources of this saltwater. The term "saltwater encroachment" is used specifically to describe the gradual lateral movement of saltwater along the base of the aquifer from the sea as a result of decreases of the freshwater head in the aquifer relative to sea level. In most instances as water from the Gulf intrudes or encroaches into an aquifer, it becomes mixed with freshwater so this water is referred to as saltwater rather than seawater. The term "seawater" is reserved for water that has a chemical composition similar to seawater. The term "saltwater front" is used to describe the leading edge of a body of saltwater in an aquifer, generally near its base. Most frequently this term is applied to saltwater that has laterally encroached from the Gulf of Mexico. The "saltwater interface" is the zone of mixing of freshwater and saltwater at the periphery of a body of encroached or intruded saltwater.

## Purpose and Scope

This report documents the relevant findings of the NE1, which evaluated monitoring in Lee and Collier Counties. The history of saltwater intrusion and the development of the saltwater intrusion monitoring network in southwest Florida are described. A detailed network improvement plan is proposed for monitoring the surficial aquifer system in the Big Cypress Basin that addresses the following:

- Design, construction, condition, and documentation of monitoring wells

- Sampling or monitoring methodologies

- Evaluation of the sources of saltwater

- Characterization of the hydrostratigraphy

- Spatial coverage of monitoring sites

- Data accessibility

- Quality assurance

Prioritization of network improvements is described. This proposed plan is designed to address all of the previously stated deficiencies in the existing network and to take advantage of recent advancements in technology that can improve the quality of monitoring.

As part of the NE1, monitoring efforts in the water-table, lower Tamiami, sandstone, mid-Hawthorn, lower Hawthorn, and Floridan aquifers in Lee and Collier Counties are considered and evaluated. The current study documents some of the findings of this broader examination, but the proposed network improvement plan is designed specifically for the surficial aquifer system, which includes the water-table and lower Tamiami aquifers of the Big Cypress Basin.

## Description of the Study Area

The study area is the 2,500 square mile (mi$^2$) Big Cypress Basin of the SFWMD (South Florida Water Management District, 2010), which includes all of Collier County and a small part of Monroe County. Prior to urban development, the Big Cypress Swamp covered most of Collier County, except the northernmost part of the county, which consisted of sandy flatwoods, and the coastal margins, which were covered by salt-tolerant mangrove marshes (fig. 4). As population increased, urbanization spread to areas that were Big Cypress Swamp, sandy flatwoods, or coastal mangrove marshes.

Land-surface altitudes range from about 1 to 2 feet (ft) in south and southwest coastal Collier County to approximately 40 ft in northern Collier County, north of Immokalee. A little less than half of the county has a land-surface altitude of less than 10 ft. A low coastal ridge in western Collier County has an altitude of approximately 10 to 17 ft. The city of Naples Coastal Ridge well field was constructed on or just east of this ridge (fig. 1).

## Hydrogeologic Setting

Currently, there are a number of interpretations of the hydrostratigraphy of the Big Cypress Basin. The hydrostratigraphic interpretation depicted in figure 5A is a combination of the hydrostratigraphic interpretation of Schmerge (2001), the "historical" interpretation of hydrostratigraphy described by BEM Systems Inc. (2003, p. 12), and the interpretations of DuBar (1991) and Missimer (2001). Historically, the aquifers of southwest Florida have been divided into the surficial aquifer system, the intermediate aquifer system, and the Floridan aquifer system (fig. 5A; Southeastern Geological Society Ad Hoc Committee on Florida Hydrostratigraphic Unit Definition, 1986). The surficial aquifer system includes two aquifers: the water-table aquifer and the lower Tamiami aquifer. The intermediate aquifer system includes the sandstone and mid-Hawthorn aquifers. Where the lower Tamiami and sandstone aquifers are not confined, they have historically been considered to be part of the water-table aquifer (BEM Systems Inc., 2003).

BEM Systems Inc. (2003) implemented an alternate hydrostratigraphic interpretation that was "developed with rules that better reflect continuity of geologic and hydrogeologic layers rather than based on the presence or absence of a confining unit." BEM Systems Inc. (2003) defined a series of hydrostratigraphic units designated "aquifer layers" and "aquitard layers" associated with specific stratigraphic units (fig. 5B; table 1). The hydrostratigraphic interpretation of BEM Systems Inc. (2003) was used for the development of some of the hydrologic models in southwest Florida, such as the Regional MIKE SHE model developed for the Southwest Florida Feasibility Study (Clyde Dabbs, South Florida Water Management District, written commun., September 28, 2012) and the Picayune Strand Restoration PIR Mike She\ Mike 11 Model (U.S. Army Corps of Engineers, and the South Florida Water Management District, 2004; Kent Feng, South Florida Water Management District, written commun., September 28, 2012).

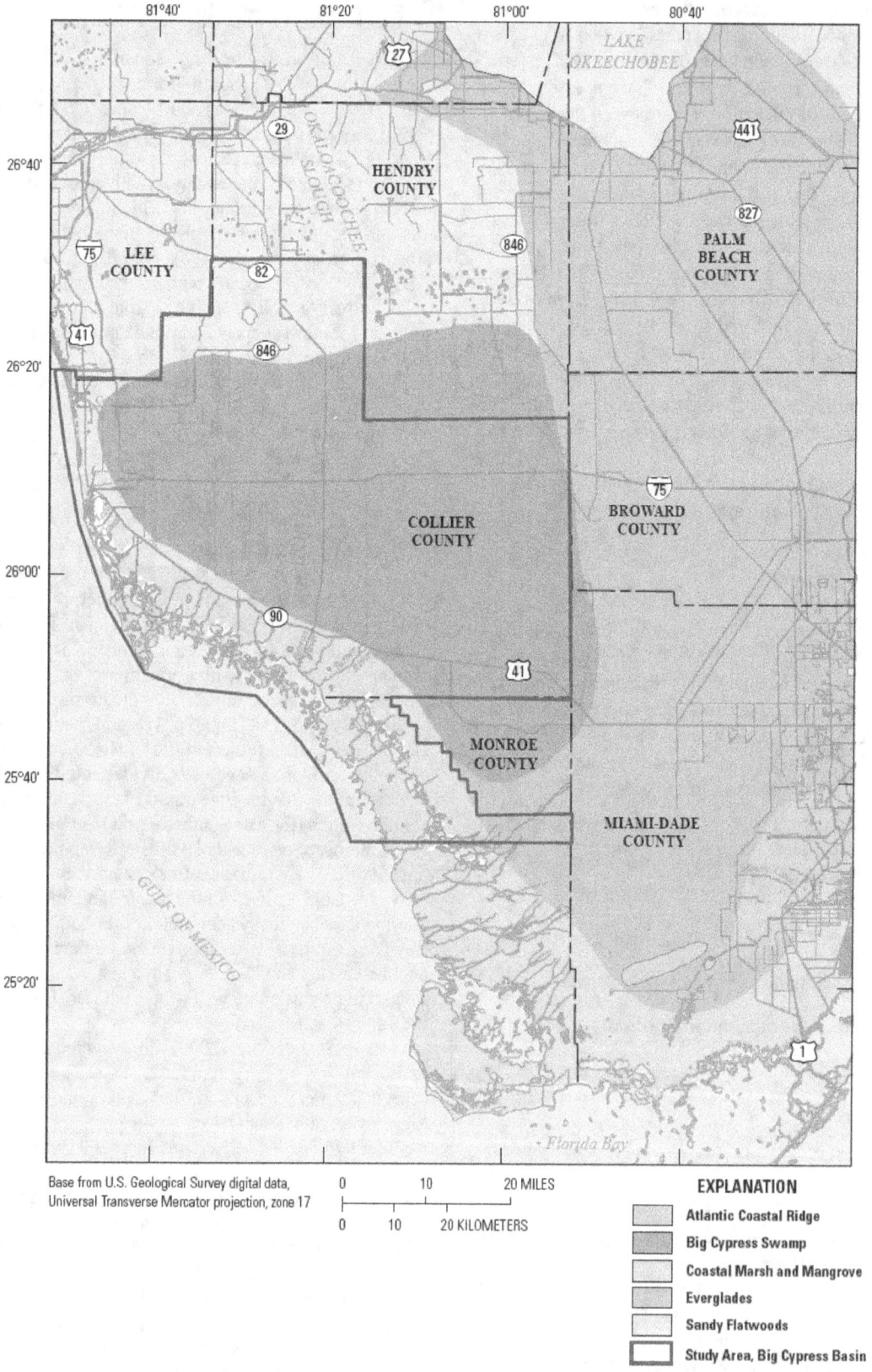

**Figure 4.** Study area and the physiographic provinces in southwest Florida. Modified from McPherson and Halley (1996).

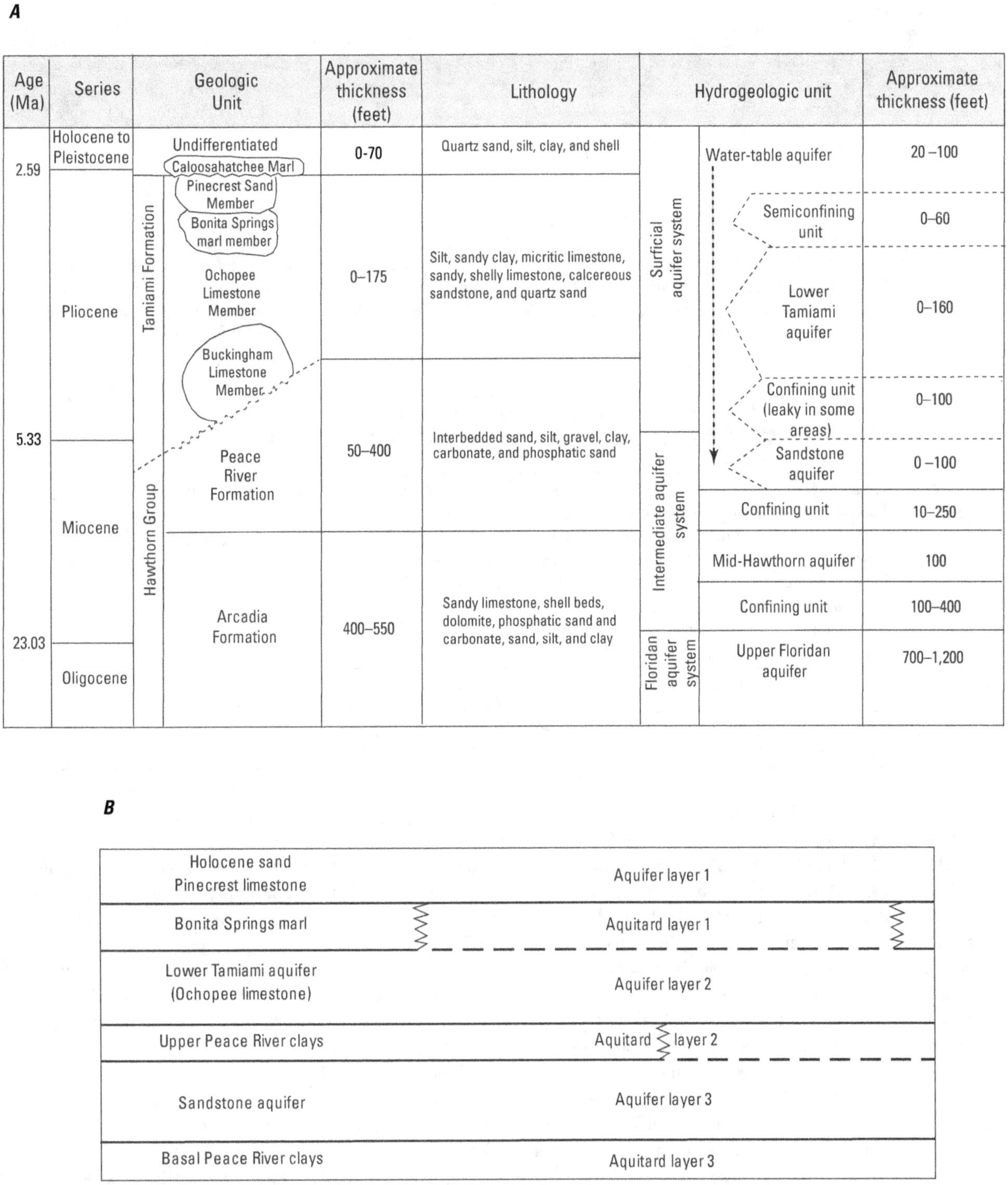

*A*

| Age (Ma) | Series | Geologic Unit | Approximate thickness (feet) | Lithology | Hydrogeologic unit | Approximate thickness (feet) |
|---|---|---|---|---|---|---|
| 2.59 | Holocene to Pleistocene | Undifferentiated / Caloosahatchee Marl | 0-70 | Quartz sand, silt, clay, and shell | Water-table aquifer (Surficial aquifer system) | 20–100 |
|  | Pliocene (Tamiami Formation) | Pinecrest Sand Member / Bonita Springs marl member | 0–175 | Silt, sandy clay, micritic limestone, sandy, shelly limestone, calcereous sandstone, and quartz sand | Semiconfining unit | 0–60 |
|  |  | Ochopee Limestone Member |  |  | Lower Tamiami aquifer | 0–160 |
|  |  | Buckingham Limestone Member |  |  | Confining unit (leaky in some areas) | 0–100 |
| 5.33 | Miocene (Hawthorn Group) | Peace River Formation | 50–400 | Interbedded sand, silt, gravel, clay, carbonate, and phosphatic sand | Sandstone aquifer (Intermediate aquifer system) | 0–100 |
|  |  |  |  |  | Confining unit | 10–250 |
|  |  |  |  |  | Mid-Hawthorn aquifer | 100 |
|  |  | Arcadia Formation | 400–550 | Sandy limestone, shell beds, dolomite, phosphatic sand and carbonate, sand, silt, and clay | Confining unit | 100–400 |
| 23.03 | Oligocene |  |  |  | Upper Floridan aquifer (Floridan aquifer system) | 700–1,200 |

*B*

| | |
|---|---|
| Holocene sand / Pinecrest limestone | Aquifer layer 1 |
| Bonita Springs marl | Aquitard layer 1 |
| Lower Tamiami aquifer (Ochopee limestone) | Aquifer layer 2 |
| Upper Peace River clays | Aquitard layer 2 |
| Sandstone aquifer | Aquifer layer 3 |
| Basal Peace River clays | Aquitard layer 3 |

**Figure 5.** Hydrostratigraphic interpretations considered during the current study. *A*, Generalized geology and hydrology of southwest Florida (modified from Schmerge, 2001). *B*, Definition of aquifers for modeling of aquifers (from BEM Systems Inc., 2003).

**Table 1.**   Description of hydrostratigraphic units defined by BEM Systems Inc., 2003, and equivalent geologic and hydrogeologic names used by the U.S. Geological Survey.

| Layer name | Description by BEM Systems, Inc. (2003) | Equivalent geologic (and hydrogeologic) names used by the U.S. Geological Survey |
|---|---|---|
| Aquifer Layer 1 | Holocene to Pleistocene sands and Late Pliocene (Pinecrest) limestone where present. | Undifferentiated Holocene to Pleistocene deposits and/or Pinecrest Sand Member of the Tamiami Formation (water table aquifer) |
| Aquitard Layer 1 | Bonita Springs Marl and Caloosahatchee Clay, where present. | Bonita Springs marl member of the Tamiami Formation (Tamiami confining unit from Reese and Cunningham, 2000 ) and/or Caloosahatchee Marl . |
| Aquifer Layer 2 | Early Pliocene (Ochopee Limestone). This unit conforms to the historical definition of lower Tamiami aquifer where confined and to the lower part of the water-table aquifer where unconfined. The vertical extent of the unit is defined from the top of Ochopee Limestone to the top of the Peace River Formation. The unit is missing in the northern part of the study area and outcrops in the southern part of the study area. | Ochopee Limestone Member of the Tamiami Formation, and potentially  permeable portions of the Buckingham Limestone Member and medium to coarse unnamed sand of the Tamiami or Peace River Formations (lower Tamiami aquifer where confined or water-table aquifer if unconfined.) |
| Aquitard Layer 2 | Upper clays in Miocene Peace River Formation, referred to locally as the Cape Coral Clay. Clays between the base of the Ochopee Limestone and top of the Miocene were included in this unit. | Upper part of the Peace River Formation, where imperiable. |
| Aquifer Layer 3 | Sandstone aquifer. This unit is defined from the top of the first sandstone unit (Lehigh Acres Sandstone) in the Peace River Formation to the top of the basal clay in the Peace River Formation. This definition conforms to the historical definition of the Sandstone aquifer except where the formation is unconfined. The Sandstone aquifer contains clay beds within the aquifer. Total thickness of sandstone and internal clay were calculated from WRS [Water Resources Solutions Inc.] data. The unit outcrops in the northern part of the study area where the Tamiami Formation is missing. | Middle Peace River Formation (sandstone aquifer where confined or water-table aquifer if unconfined.) |
| Aquitard Layer 3 | Basal clays in the Peace River Formation, referred to locally as the Fort Myers Clay. The unit extends vertically to the top of the Arcadia Formation, which we [BEM Systems Inc. (2003)] presumed to be equivalent to the top of the Mid-Hawthorn aquifer. | Basal part of the Peace River Formation. |

The hydrostratigraphic interpretation of BEM Systems Inc. (2003) is based on a compilation of existing information from the Bureau of Oil and Gas (BOG), Florida Geological Survey (FGS), SFWMD, USGS, and private firms, including available information from the SFWMD's Well Inventory and Lithological Geophysical Maintenance Application (WILMA) database (now incorporated into SFWMD's DBHYDRO database (South Florida Water Management, 2012)) and the Water Resources Solutions, Inc. (WRS) database. DBHYDRO also includes much of the stratigraphic information from the files of the USGS. These sources provided more information than was available for the hydrostratigraphic interpretations of Knapp and others (1986) in Collier County and Wedderburn and others (1982) in Lee County. The hydrostratigraphic cross sections depicted in this report are based on the hydrostratigraphic interpretation of BEM Systems Inc. (2003). The construction of these cross sections is described in greater detail in the section "Lower Tamiami Aquifer."

Although the hydrostratigraphic interpretation of BEM Systems Inc. (2003) has defined aquifers and aquitards based on "continuity of geologic and hydrogeologic layers," the hydrostratigraphy of the aquifers in southwest Florida can be more complex. Confining units or "aquitards" may be absent, and strata that are poorly transmissive in some areas may be transmissive in other areas. The water-table aquifer generally consists of undifferentiated deposits and the upper part of the Tamiami Formation of Pliocene age (Reese, 2000, p. 21) including the Pinecrest Sand Member (Hunter, 1968). In most areas, a confining unit consisting of the Caloosahatchee Marl or Bonita Springs marl member of the Tamaimi Formation lies between the water-table and lower Tamiami aquifers, (fig. 5A; table 1; BEM Systems Inc., 2003). Where the Bonita Springs marl member of the Tamiami Formation (Missimer, 1993) and Caloosahatchee Marl (fig. 5A; Missimer, 1993) are absent, however, the lower Tamiami aquifer and the water-table aquifer become one aquifer.

The lower Tamiami aquifer generally coincides with the strata of the lower part of the Tamiami Formation including the Buckingham Limestone Member (DuBar, 1991) and Ochopee Limestone Member (DuBar, 1991). In some areas, however, the lower Tamiami or water-table aquifers extend downward into unconsolidated coarse siliciclastics at the top of the Peace River Formation (Reese, 2000, p. 21) of the Hawthorn Group (fig. 5A).

A confining unit is generally present between the surficial aquifer system and the intermediate aquifer system; in some areas this confining unit is thin and leaky (Campbell, 1988; Shoemaker and Edwards 2003). The sandstone aquifer includes the permeable sand and sandstone strata of the Peace River Formation and is separated from the underlying mid-Hawthorn aquifer by clayey dolosilts, locally interbedded with thin seams of porous limestone, sand, and dolomites (Wedderburn and others, 1982). The mid-Hawthorn aquifer includes the upper part of the Arcadia Formation (fig. 5*A*).

It is beyond the scope of the current study to evaluate the hydrostratigraphic interpretation of BEM Systems Inc. (2003), but the differences between the hydrostratigraphic interpretation of BEM Systems Inc. (2003) depicted in figure 5*B* and that of previous researchers (fig. 5*A*) may have led to inconsistencies that are described in subsequent sections of this report, such as differences in the classification of wells by aquifer. The organizations conducting monitoring in southwest Florida have generally classified the monitoring wells by the aquifer to which the well is open. These classifications may have followed the interpretations depicted in figures 5*A*, 5*B*, or possibly some of the older hydrostratigraphic interpretations that have been developed for this area. It was beyond the scope of the current study to reclassify each well by aquifer, but some of the discrepancies observed during the analysis have been noted. The hydrostratigraphic interpretation of BEM Systems Inc. (2003) was delineated using a different set of rules than previous interpretations; therefore, the remaining text of this report denotes when hydrostratigraphic interpretation of BEM Systems Inc. (2003) is being used or discussed.

# Saltwater Intrusion in South Florida

Improvement of saltwater intrusion monitoring strategies requires an understanding of the mechanisms and history that led to the present-day distribution and extent of saltwater in the aquifers of south Florida. Incorrect interpretation of the origin of saltwater in a given area may lead to implementation of remediation or preventative measures that do not prevent the saltwater from intruding. Continual monitoring, for example, of a mass of saltwater that leaked from a canal decades ago and is slowly dissipating is generally not as useful as monitoring saltwater that is currently moving along the base of the aquifer toward the intakes of a well field. If the mechanisms and history of saltwater intrusion within the study area are understood, this knowledge can be used to effectively direct monitoring activities.

## Mechanisms of Saltwater Intrusion

Beginning in the early 1940s, USGS studies conducted in south Florida identified the following causes of saltwater intrusion: (1) lateral encroachment of saltwater along the base of aquifers caused by reductions in freshwater head by water-supply withdrawals or canal drainage (Cross and Love, 1942, p. 501); (2) infiltration from tidal marshes, estuaries, and bays; (3) the migration of saltwater upstream in unregulated canals or streams during drought periods and the leakage of this water into the surficial aquifer system (Cross and Love, 1942, p. 501; Parker and others, 1955); (4) movement of residual saltwater that entered the aquifer during previous sea-level high stands of interglacial periods (Matson and Stanford, 1913, p. 261; Parker, 1945, p. 533); and (5) upward seepage through leaky confining units and poorly sealed wells (McCoy, 1962, 1972) (fig. 6).

These mechanisms of saltwater intrusion have combined or overlapped to create the current distribution of saltwater in the aquifers of southwest Florida. It is difficult to differentiate between the various sources of saltwater because some areas may have been intruded by multiple sources of saltwater. For example, saltwater that has leaked from a canal may sink to the base of the aquifer and combine with saltwater that is gradually encroaching from the Gulf of Mexico, or saltwater that is leaking upward from a deeper aquifer through the casing of a corroded well. Episodes of contamination from multiple sources may increase the difficulty of determining the source of saltwater.

Sea-level rise may exacerbate saltwater intrusion by increasing saltwater encroachment along the base of the aquifer as a result of a decrease in freshwater head relative to sea level or enhanced leakage of saltwater from surface-water features. On the basis of data collected between 1965 and 2006, the National Oceanic and Atmospheric Administration (NOAA) estimated that mean sea level at Key West, Naples, and Ft. Myers, Florida, increased, respectively, at rates of 0.7, 0.7, and 0.8 ft per 100 years (National Oceanic and Atmospheric Administration, 2012). Some predictions of sea-level rise for this area suggest an increasing rate of rise (Intergovernmental Panel on Climate Change, 2007; South Florida Water Management District, 2009). Even given current rates of sea-level rise, the potential for saltwater intrusion is increasing.

## Effects of Surface-Water Drainage

Much of the saltwater intrusion in southwest Florida is a consequence of changes to the hydrology of this area during the late 19th and early to mid-20th centuries. Surface water in the Big Cypress Swamp once flowed predominantly southward through the Okaloacoochee Slough and Fakahatchee Strand (fig. 4; Swayze and McPherson, 1977). The first major change to the drainage of southwest Florida was the extension of a drainage canal from Lake Okeechobee to the Caloosahatchee River (fig. 1) in 1888, which reversed the groundwater gradient near the river and reduced southerly flow through Okaloacoochee Slough and Fakahatchee Strand (fig. 4; Swayze and McPherson, 1977). Drainage canals associated with State Road 29 (fig. 1) completed in 1926, and the Tamiami Trail (U.S. Highway 41; fig. 1) completed

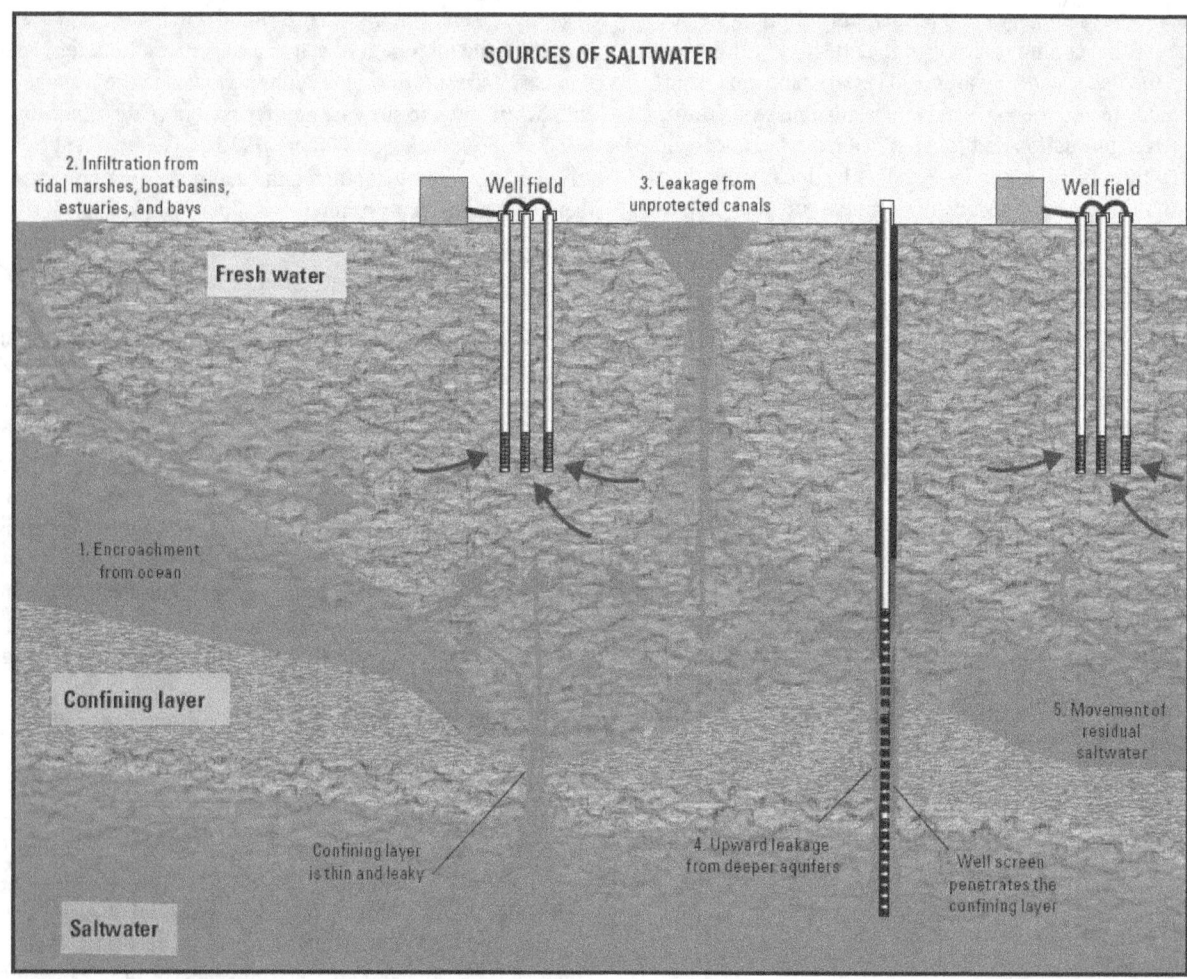

**Figure 6.**   The saltwater in the aquifers of southwest Florida has entered these aquifers through various pathways, including (1) encroachment from the ocean, (2) infiltration from tidal marshes, estuaries, and bays, (3) leakage from unprotected canals, (4) upward leakage from deeper aquifers, and (5) movement of residual saltwater from previous sea-level high stands.

in 1928, re-routed and increased drainage in the Big Cypress Basin. Drainage canals and boat basins were installed to drain land and allow navigational access to the Gulf of Mexico (Klein, 1954; fig. 1). In Naples, the boat basins and drainage canals led to saltwater intrusion within the aquifer south of Broad Avenue (Klein, 1954, p. 32) (fig. 1). Klein (1954) found that on September 2 and October 2, 1951, seawater had flowed up the Gordon River (fig. 1) and caused salty water to flow laterally into the water-table aquifer. McCoy (1962) reported that saltwater from the Gordon River had infiltrated downward into the aquifer to a depth of 25 ft below land surface (bls) and had reportedly caused the loss of several rows of litchi trees near the river in the Caribbean Botanical Gardens (fig.1). McCoy (1962, p. 54) noted that saltwater had moved inland beneath the Gordon River, presumably as a result of local lowering of the groundwater level in the adjacent drainage area.

Drainage increased during the 1960s when the major drainage canals were installed, including (1) borrow canals adjacent to State Road 846 and County Road 856, (2) the Cocohatchee Canal adjacent to State Road 846 (also called Immokalee Road), (3) a borrow canal adjacent to State Road 856 that is no longer evident in maps of the drainage system, (4) a canal that runs around the perimeter of the Naples Airport and into Naples Bay, (5) extension of the natural Henderson Creek (fig. 4) that is connected to the borrow ditch along County Road 951 (fig. 1), (6) the Golden Gate Canal system (fig. 4), consisting of approximately 70 mi of canals in a 120 mi$^2$ area, and (7) the installation of the FAKA Union Canal System (fig. 4) in central Collier County in what had once been the western portion of the Big Cypress Swamp (South Florida Water Management District, 2006; Swayze and McPherson, 1977). These drainage efforts lowered water levels in the Big Cypress Basin and allowed saltwater to encroach inland along the bases of the water-table and lower Tamiami aquifers. To mitigate saltwater intrusion, salinity control structures were installed in most of the canals that lead to the coast. These structures prevent saltwater from flowing inland where it can leak into the aquifer and increase the hydraulic head both in the canals and the aquifer adjacent to the canals, which reduces the potential for saltwater encroachment along the bases of the aquifers.

## Effects of Groundwater Withdrawals

Water levels in the surficial aquifer were reduced by the withdrawals of municipal water supply well fields. This decline became evident in 1945 when the city of Naples well field, consisting of three closely spaced and heavily pumped wells located between Naples Bay and the Gulf of Mexico (Sherwood and Klein, 1961, p. 8) became salty and had to be abandoned (Klein, 1954, p. 2). In the mid-1940s the city of Naples installed a new municipal water supply well field further north that included 22, 3- and 4-inch-diameter wells spaced about 400 ft apart (McCoy, 1962, p. 33). Klein (1954, p. 32) noted that during the dry season, water levels near this well field could be reduced to a level that would allow saltwater encroachment on a broad front. In 1954, new public water-supply wells were installed in the area between the Atlantic Coast Railway Line (now Goodlette-Frank Road) and the Gordon River and between 500 and 1,400 ft north of Caribbean Gardens (fig. 1; McCoy, 1962, p. 33–34). In 1962, McCoy (1962, p. 58) indicated that a water supply could be developed in northwestern Collier County on the eastern side of the coastal ridge. The city of Naples Coastal Ridge well field was installed in this area. In 1967 the USGS was requested to identify areas farther inland that would provide sufficient water quality for public water supply (McCoy, 1972, p. 3). The Collier County Public Water Supply Golden Gate and city of Naples East Golden Gate well fields were installed in the areas identified. The city of Naples Coastal Ridge well field is still in operation, but increasing chloride concentration of water samples from wells C-489 ,C-516, C-525, and C-526 (fig. 3) likely indicates that the saltwater from the Gulf of Mexico is encroaching farther inland in this area.

## Residual Saltwater

Klein (1954), Sherwood and Klein (1961), McCoy (1962), Klein (1980), and Schmerge (2001) described areas within the Big Cypress Basin of brackish or highly mineralized groundwater not associated with recent saltwater intrusion. Klein (1954, p. 35) indicated that the brackish water in the shallow non-artesian aquifer is residual seawater of Pleistocene age trapped in sediments of lower permeability. McCoy (1962) created a cross section showing the extent of brackish water in low permeability strata extending from just east of the Naples Coastal Ridge well field to about 10 mi inland. He also indicated that because groundwater altitudes in the area range from 5 to 15 ft, this saltwater could not be associated with

recent encroachment from the Gulf of Mexico. McCoy (1962, p. 55) noted the presence of brackish water in the shallow aquifer extending 10 mi east of the Naples Coastal Ridge well field but that the shallow aquifer 15 mi east of the Naples area appeared to contain large quantities of groundwater that was similar in quality to that of coastal areas.

## Upward Leakage of Saltwater

Klein (1980, p. 22) indicated that a possible source of saltwater in the area east of Naples is upward leakage of artesian water from the Floridan aquifer system or through open well bores or corroded casings of artesian wells. Schmerge (2001) analyzed samples from wells in the aquifers of Lee and Collier Counties for strontium isotopes and found that the strontium-87/strontium-86 ratio in water from some of wells open to the lower Tamiami aquifer resembled that of water from the sandstone, mid-Hawthorn, lower Hawthorn, and even Floridan aquifers. Shoemaker and Edwards (2003, p. 1) modeled the lower Tamiami aquifer just north of Collier County in the vicinity of the Bonita Springs well field and concluded that upconing of saltwater through the semiconfining layers at the base of the lower Tamiami aquifer was of utmost concern and that lateral encroachment of saltwater was of second-most concern.

## Delineation of Saltwater Intrusion

Several studies have delineated the extent of saltwater intrusion in the surficial aquifer in and around the Big Cypress Basin. Knapp and others (1986) and Schmerge (2001) provided maps showing saltwater content in the lower Tamiami aquifer. Knapp and others (1986) found that chloride concentration in the lower Tamiami aquifer ranged from less than 5 mg/L to more than 10,000 mg/L, with the highest values occurring along the coast. Knapp and others (1986) also found that immediately south of Bonita Springs, chloride values ranged from 100 to 500 mg/L, which they considered to have been caused by saltwater intrusion associated with the Cocohatchee Canal (fig. 4). Another area of saltwater intrusion near the Henderson Creek Canal was also identified (Knapp and others, 1986). In 2011, the SFWMD created maps showing the landward extent of the 250-mg/L isochlor in the water-table and lower Tamiami aquifers (figs. 1-1, 1-2) based on salinity data collected from the JSWIM network monitoring wells in April and May 2009.

One concern with these maps is that many of the monitoring wells used do not fully penetrate the aquifer, so there was no way of determining the chloride concentration of the water at the base of the aquifer. Another concern is that it is difficult to differentiate between leakage of saltwater from canals or rivers, recent saltwater encroachment along the base of the aquifer, upward leakage of saltwater from deeper aquifers, or pre-existing saltwater when the only results available from groundwater samples are measurements of total dissolved solids, chloride concentration, and specific conductivity.

# Joint Saltwater Intrusion Monitoring Network Description and Examination

The JSWIM network, depicted in figure 7, was evaluated during the NE1. This network includes approximately 1,600 sites. The city of Cape Coral, the CCPCPD, LCNRD, and the USGS monitored about 30 percent of the sites of the JSWIM network (fig. 7). Seventy percent of the sites were monitored under the auspices of the SFWMD-SWIMM program. As withdrawals from the aquifers of southwest Florida and the information required to evaluate the effects of these withdrawals increased the JSWIM network gradually expanded to provide necessary monitoring.

## Network Development and Evaluations

During 1937–1990 the USGS developed a cooperative monitoring network (USGS-COOP-SWIM) in southwest Florida. The size of this network varied from 0 to 59 wells, and averaged 14 wells during 1937–1972. This monitoring included several reconnaissance efforts to evaluate freshwater resources. Between 1973 and 1990 the network was increased to include a maximum of 330 sites. Existing domestic, industrial, irrigation, or water-supply wells were monitored to evaluate freshwater resources and saltwater intrusion. Most of these wells were not ideally suited for saltwater intrusion monitoring because they did not fully penetrate the aquifer and had long open intervals. A limited number of test wells were installed to evaluate the water quality and stratigraphy of deeper parts of the aquifer. The test well C-123 (formerly designated well "123") is one of the only wells that fully penetrates the lower Tamiami aquifer near the city of Naples Coastal Ridge well field. These test wells were widely distributed throughout the county and were used for a variety of hydrologic and stratigraphic evaluations.

In 1980, a cooperative USGS and the Big Cypress Basin Board study (Klein, 1980) identified a number of deficiencies in available hydrologic information including (1) poor delineation of the extent of saltwater intrusion along the southern coastal area, (2) inadequate information concerning the areal extent and depth of the bottom of the shallow aquifer, and (3) insufficient groundwater quality information for most of Collier County except near Naples, an area of mineralized water east of Naples, and an area further inland that was being explored as a future water supply for the city of Naples (Klein, 1980). Klein (1980, p. 23) described the need for (1) replacement of wells that had been destroyed, (2) new monitoring wells that bracket the position of water containing 500 mg/L of chloride near the base of the aquifer, and (3) new monitoring wells that monitor the bases of the water-table and lower Tamiami aquifers.

A subsection of the USGS-COOP-SWIM network, consisting of 74 wells jointly supported by the SFWMD and the USGS in Collier County, was examined by Burns and Shih (1984) to classify all the existing USGS monitoring wells by aquifer, and identify any major gaps and redundancies The network analysis resulted in a recommendation of an additional 62 monitoring wells, and discontinuation of 7 of the original USGS-COOP-SWIM network wells. Their analysis also noted that the SFWMD-SWIMM network consisted primarily of wells that were "clustered around the well field" (p. 41) whereas the USGS-COOP-SWIM network "monitors the regional flow system" (p. 41). Eventually, new wells were installed at most of the locations recommended by Burns and Shih (1984), and monitored under the USGS-COOP-SWIM program. The data from these wells improved the water-level monitoring spatial coverage but did not address most of the issues raised by Klein (1980).

In 1994, the USGS-COOP-SWIM monitoring program was reduced from 296 to 57 surface-water and groundwater monitoring sites. Another network examination was conducted by the South Florida Water Management District (Hosung Ahn, written commun., June 1996) to evaluate reductions in the groundwater-level monitoring part of the USGS network. This examination did not affect the remaining USGS-COOP-SWIM monitoring sites, but did spur a new study to reevaluate the network while also considering trends in water levels and salinity. This new study began during the drought of 1998–2002 (Abtew and others, 2003; Verdi and others, 2006). During this study: (1) the USGS-COOP-SWIM network was temporarily expanded for the duration of the drought using wells that had previously been discontinued, (2) trends in water-level and salinity were evaluated, (3) a real-time water level monitoring network was designed and implemented, and (4) a Web-based data analysis package was developed that included graphical and statistical evaluations of water levels and salinity (Prinos and others, 2002; U.S. Geological Survey, 2012a). The evaluation of trends in salinity using chloride concentration data collected during the period 1974 to 1999 indicated upward trends in chloride concentration of 1.5, 2.8, 8.9, 0.5, 7, and 1.1 mg/L per year, respectively, in samples from wells C-489, C-492, C-525, C-528, C-977, and C-998 (fig. 1), which are open to the lower Tamiami aquifer (fig. 5A), and increases of about +1 mg/L per year during respective 15- and 12-year periods, from wells C-953 and C-1063 (fig. 1), open to the water-table aquifer (fig. 5A, Prinos and others, 2002). No permanent additions were made to the USGS-COOP-SWIM network.

## Recent Monitoring (2007–2008)

The NE1 required the compilation of data from the city of Cape Coral, the CCPCPD, the Florida Department of Environmental Protection (FDEP), the LCNRD, the SFWMD, and the USGS collected in southwest Florida (Lee and Collier Counties) during the period 2007–2008. Data from approximately 1,600 monitoring sites had been collected by these organizations during this period to evaluate the salinity of surface-water bodies, the water-table aquifer, the lower Tamiami

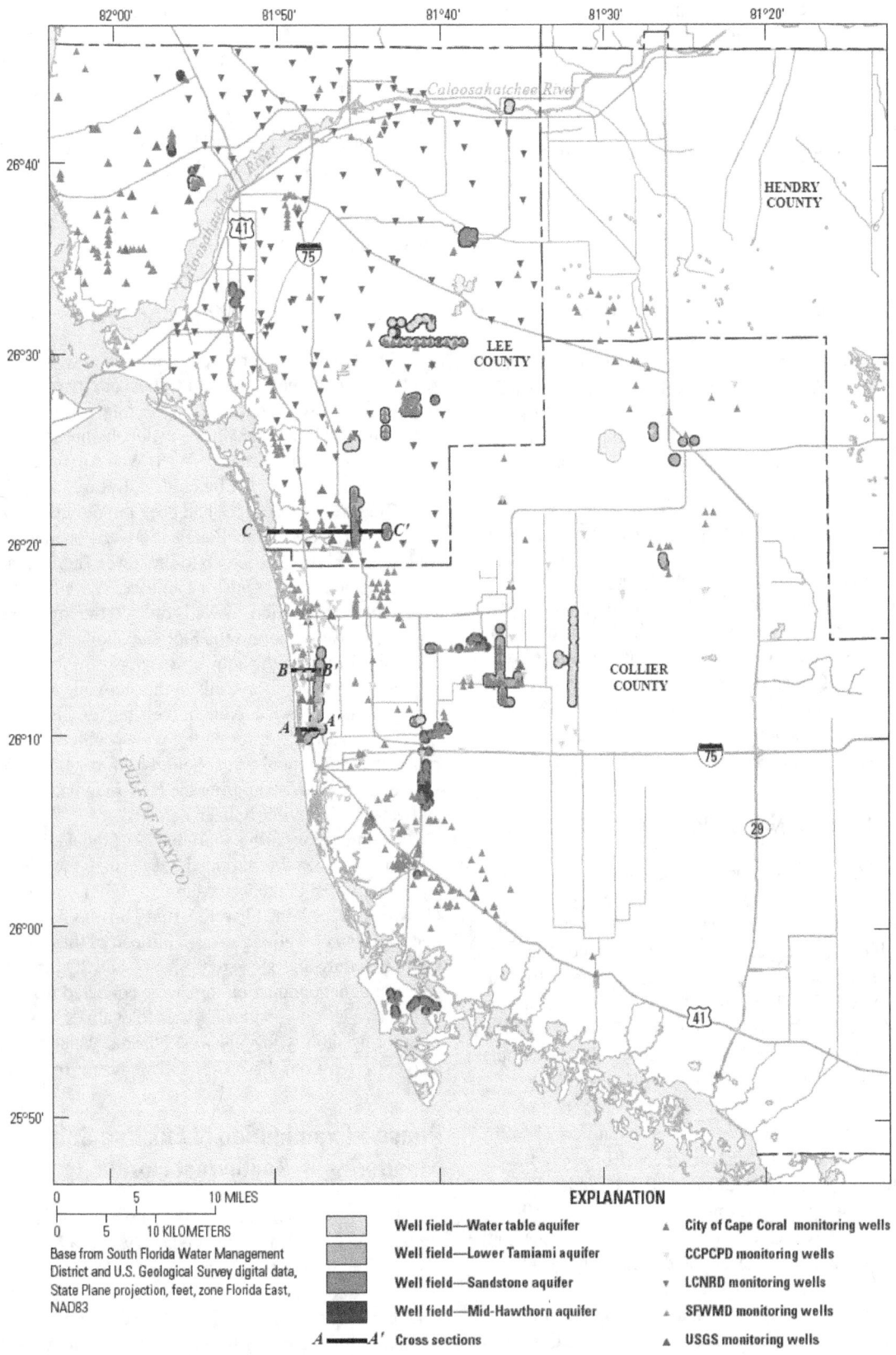

**Figure 7.**  Joint Saltwater Intrusion Monitoring (JSWIM) Network in southwest Florida.

aquifer, the sandstone aquifer, the mid-Hawthorn aquifer, the lower Hawthorn aquifer, and the Floridan aquifer system (fig. 7). Some wells are monitored by multiple agencies or the data collected from them are stored in multiple databases.

## Collier County Pollution Control and Prevention Department

The CCPCPD network is designed for pollution detection rather than saltwater intrusion monitoring; however, the water samples or measurements collected are evaluated for specific conductance and chloride concentration. During January 23, 2007 to July 24, 2007, the CCPCPD collected samples and (or) measurements from 75 surface-water sites and 71 wells, (table 2-1). Fifty-four of the wells sampled are listed as being screened in the surficial aquifer system. Only 17 wells are screened in deeper aquifers, including 10 in the lower Tamiami, 4 in the mid-Hawthorn, and 3 in the sandstone.

## Florida Department of Environmental Protection

Data from the FDEP are available through the FDEP STORET online database utility (Florida Department of Environmental Protection, 2012) and the U.S. Environmental Protection Agency (USEPA) STORET data warehouse. Data stored in the FDEP STORET database for the period 2007–2008 included results of water quality sampling of 75 sites surface-water sites (table 2-2), and 87 groundwater wells. Almost all of these sites were monitored by the CCPCPD.

## SFWMD-SWIMM Network

The SFWMD-SWIMM network includes wells monitored by water-use permittees. Salinity data collected by numerous organizations, including private and public water supply utilities, golf courses, agricultural interests, and communities, were provided by the SFWMD as a series of tables retrieved from the SFWMD-SALT database. One of the most common evaluations of water salinity available from SFWMD-SWIMM network sites was the chloride concentration of water samples, so this constituent was used for the NE1. The SFWMD-SWIMM network included data from 1,143 sites (table 2-3), including 171 wells open to the water-table aquifer, 96 wells open to the surficial aquifer system, 252 wells open to the lower Tamiami aquifer, 101 wells open to the sandstone aquifer, 190 wells open to the mid-Hawthorn aquifer, 198 wells open to the lower Hawthorn aquifer, 45 wells open to the Floridan aquifer, and 90 surface-water monitoring sites (data collected January 1, 2007, to December 31, 2008).

Most of the 96 wells classified as being open to the surficial aquifer system were located in central Lee County at the Lee County Utilities Corkscrew well field, and in southern Collier County south of I-75 and near U.S. Highway 41. Based on the hydrostratigraphic interpretation of BEM Systems Inc. (2003), most of these wells are open to "Aquifer Layer 2" which generally corresponds to the lower Tamiami aquifer (fig. 5B; table 1). Some of these wells in the Lee County Utilities Corkscrew well field, however, are open to "Aquifer Layer 3" which generally corresponds to the sandstone aquifer (fig. 5B; table 1). Data from wells 302D and 323D sampled in January and February of 2011 by the city of Naples are also included because data from these wells were not available in the retrieval from the SFWMD-SALT database yet these data are important to evaluating saltwater intrusion near the city of Naples Coastal Ridge well field.

## USGS Cooperative Monitoring Network

The USGS Cooperative Monitoring network includes wells that are owned by local utilities, or city or county organizations. Well construction information, if available, and data collected by the USGS are available through the National Water Information System (NWIS) Web database (U.S. Geological Survey, 2012b) or by request. In Lee and Collier Counties, 636 groundwater sites had been monitored for salinity by the USGS since 1975, including 155 wells open to the water-table aquifer, 105 wells open to the lower Tamiami aquifer, 78 wells open to the sandstone aquifer, 99 wells open to the mid-Hawthorn aquifer, 55 wells open to the lower Hawthorn aquifer, 14 wells open to the Floridan aquifer system, and 130 sites for which the aquifer was not specified (table 2-4). About 40 percent of the wells in this network were only sampled once or twice. Nine of the sites for which no aquifer or well construction information was specified are water plants rather than individual wells. Salinity information from inactive USGS wells was used during the NE1 to indicate areas where saltwater had previously been detected.

Salinity monitoring at all but 29 of the wells in this network has been discontinued. Of the active wells, salinity is monitored in the water-table (5 wells), lower Tamiami (10 wells), sandstone (3 wells), mid-Hawthorn (10 wells), and Floridan (1 well) aquifers. Fourteen of these sites were in Collier County and 15 were in Lee County. During the NE1, electromagnetic induction logs were collected from six active or inactive USGS monitoring sites to evaluate this method for monitoring salinity in southwest Florida. Water samples were also collected from these sites and analyzed for salinity.

## Phase 1 Examination of Existing Salinity Monitoring in Southwest Florida

During the NE1, the JSWIM network coverage was spatially evaluated, and included analysis of (1) the spatial distribution of salinity monitoring in surface-water bodies and the water-table, lower Tamiami, sandstone, and mid-Hawthorn aquifers in Lee and Collier Counties, (2) the design of monitoring wells, (3) ambient and dynamic well-bore flow, (4) hydrostratigraphy, and (5) data-collection techniques. The distribution of monitoring sites was also compared to the locations and depths of water-supply wells (table 2-5). Findings from this analysis include:

- Surface-water salinity monitoring is insufficient in some areas to evaluate the occurrence of saltwater in some canals near coastal well fields.

- Although there are some gaps, monitoring in the water-table aquifer is generally sufficient to approximate the inland extent of saltwater in the water-table aquifer in western Collier County and southwest Lee County near the coast.

- JSWIM network wells completed in the lower Tamiami, sandstone, and mid-Hawthorn aquifers are typically too shallow for evaluation of lateral saltwater encroachment from the Gulf of Mexico along the bases of these aquifers.

- The JSWIM network includes a large percentage of public or private water-supply wells or irrigation wells that were neither designed nor intended to be used specifically for monitoring of saltwater intrusion and evaluation of the sources of saltwater.

- Existing monitoring generally is sufficient to warn water managers and utility operators if the water supply or irrigation wells are becoming contaminated by saltwater.

- Well construction information is missing for some of the JSWIM wells.

- The locations of some monitoring wells are uncertain.

- Some of the JSWIM network wells being monitored are damaged or obstructed and cannot provide information that is fully characteristic of salinity in the aquifer.

- Purging methods being used by some organizations may not provide samples that are fully characteristic of salinity in the aquifer.

- Many JSWIM network wells have very long open-borehole or long screened intervals, which may be causing variability in salinity data.

- Existing monitoring is inadequate to fully evaluate sources of saltwater.

- Some of the public water-supply wells and JSWIM network wells currently are listed as being in a different aquifer or confining unit than would be determined using the hydrostratigraphic interpretation of BEM Systems Inc. (2003).

- Some of the monitoring is redundant.

- The network is dense in some areas and sparse in others, and it does not tightly bracket the saltwater front within the lower Tamiami aquifer.

- Development of and adherence to a JSWIM network quality-assurance plan would improve the quality of information available.

- Most of the monitoring conducted is in or close to public water supply well fields or other water-supply wells.

- Some technological advances that can improve the quality of salinity monitoring are not being implemented.

To determine if the JSWIM monitoring network is still largely "clustered around the well field[s]" (Burns and Shih, 1984, p. 41), monitoring sites within 100 ft of public water-supply wells were identified. This examination revealed that, as of July 2008, 64 percent (or 675 of 1,053) groundwater monitoring wells in the SFWMD-SWIMM network were either the public water-supply wells or monitoring wells within 100 ft of the public water-supply wells. Many of the wells in the SFWMD-SWIMM network that were not within 100 ft of public water-supply wells were private water-supply wells or irrigation wells. This monitoring would likely warn water managers and utility operators if the water-supply or irrigation wells are becoming contaminated. Although the existing monitoring fulfills a specific need, if the first warning of saltwater intrusion within a well field is the contamination of the water-supply wells, it could be too late to implement measures necessary to avoid contamination.

# Analysis of Monitoring and Development of a Saltwater Intrusion Monitoring Network Improvement Plan

The proposed network improvement plan considers the current state of the existing monitoring networks, and the steps that could be taken to improve saltwater intrusion monitoring in the Big Cypress Basin. The following sections describe the well design and monitoring criteria. The JSWIM network includes many wells that are active water-supply wells. Some of the activities/steps indicated may not apply to these types of wells.

## Well Design, Construction, Documentation, and Identification

Common types of monitoring wells are (1) long- or short-screened interval wells that have a filter pack, (2) open ended wells, and (3) wells that have a long interval of open borehole (fig. 8). Variations of these designs also exist, such as screened wells without filter packs, wells that have a short interval of open borehole, or wells that have multiple open intervals.

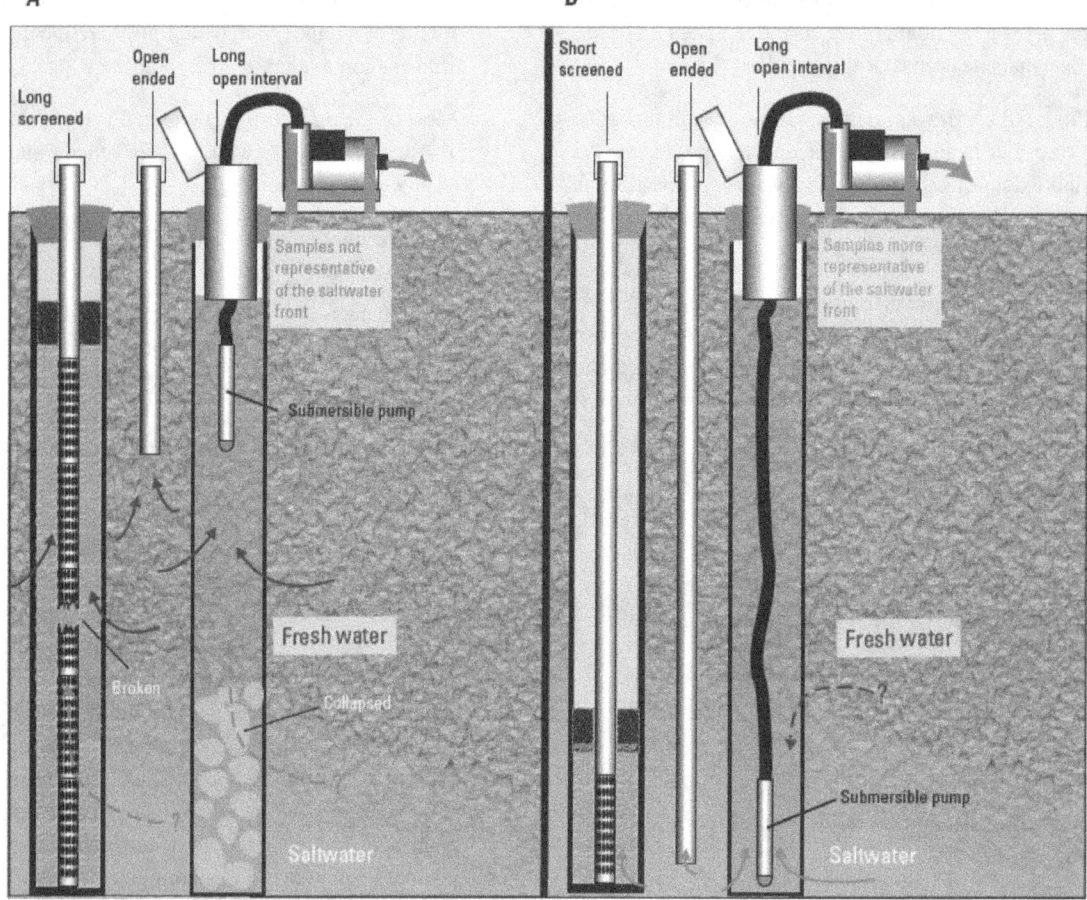

**Figure 8.** Types of monitoring wells and sampling: (*A*) Examples of wells that are unsuited for salinity monitoring. (*B*) Examples of wells that, if sampled correctly, can provide meaningful salinity results.

Some of the wells of the JSWIM were designed following USEPA and FDEP guidelines, but others were not. Guidelines for monitoring-well installation include:

- The FDEP monitoring-well design and construction guidance manual (Florida Department of Environmental Protection, 2008a).

- The USEPA handbook of suggested practices for the design and installation of groundwater-monitoring wells (U.S. Environmental Protection Agency, 1991), and

- USGS guidelines and standard procedures for studies of ground-water quality: Selection and installation of wells, and supporting documentation (Lapham and others, 1997).

Open boreholes are vulnerable to collapse; accordingly, wells with screens and filter packs would likely prolong the utility of monitoring wells in the network. The FDEP (2008a, p. 29) indicates that "each well should be constructed with a new, machine slotted or continuously wound screen section" and that "the extra cost for screen installation can be more than offset by the assurance of an unobstructed opening to the

required depth during repeated usage". Screens generally are installed with filter packs. FDEP (2008a), USEPA (1991), and Lapham and others (1997) describe the installation of filter packs that will ensure that the well will not become clogged with sediment from the aquifer.

In south Florida, wells have historically been cased with a variety of materials including black iron, stainless steel, Teflon®, or polyvinyl chloride casing (PVC). Historically, black iron was used extensively because it was a common plumbing material prior to the 1960s. Black iron or steel well casings are generally strong and resist collapse or separation, but are susceptible to corrosion in saline conditions, which has been reported for thousands of wells in southwest Florida (Boggess and others, 1977; Fitzpatrick, 1986; and La Rose, 1990). These corroded casings contributed to intrusion of saltwater into previously fresh portions of aquifers through leakage; therefore, the remaining iron and steel well casings in the JSWIM network may eventually result in additional problems if not replaced, or properly plugged and abandoned.

PVC is a better alternative to meet the needs of the JSWIM network in the surficial and intermediate aquifer systems, because of the potential for corrosion of black iron and steel casings in saline environments. If PVC casing is used, the FDEP requires that "Couplings with the casing and between the casing and the screen must be compatibly threaded. Thermal- or solvent-welded couplings on PVC shall not be used." Lapham and others (1997) indicate that threaded joints with O-rings or Teflon tape are preferable to glued joints because PVC primer and adhesives used to join sections of PVC have been shown to leach volatile organic compounds into the water.

During well installation, curing of cement used to form an annular seal can potentially generate enough heat to melt PVC casing as a result of heat of hydration (Lapham and others, 1997). The USEPA (1991, p. 100) notes that the more cement that surrounds the casing the greater the temperature increase during curing. This heat of hydration can be in excess of 170 degrees Fahrenheit for 12 inches of grout. This possibility is reduced by minimizing the amount of cement emplaced at a given time and by keeping the annular space between the casing and the wall of the boring to a minimal thickness.

PVC casings can also bend when installed, which can prevent sampling equipment or geophysical logging equipment from progressing down the well. For this reason FDEP (2008a) specifies that "riser sections should be installed as straight and level as possible" and that "for deep installations (greater than 40 feet) centralizers should be used to ensure a constant annular spacing between the borehole and well materials."

## Well Identification and Location

Clear identification or marking of a well will prevent accidental sampling of incorrect wells. FDEP guidelines indicate that "each well at a site should have a unique label that distinguishes it from all other wells located at the installation" and that "a metal tag containing the well designation should be attached to the protective casing of each monitoring well" (Florida Department of Environmental Protection, 2008a, p. 24). This practice was not always followed or, if it was, some of these metal tags are now missing from many JSWIM wells. If wells are not clearly labeled and if technicians do not have maps providing exact distances from fixed landmarks, experience has demonstrated that it is possible for the wrong well to be sampled.

During the NE1 and other recent studies, it was noted that for some wells, geographic coordinates provided by different organizations differed, in some instances by a substantial distance. For example, locations of Collier County public water-supply wells 33 and 34 were about 4 mi from the coast near U.S. Highway 41 and State Highway 951 in the 2007 retrieval of information from the SFWMD-SALT database. These wells are actually located about 17 mi inland in the Collier County Utilities Golden Gate well field. This error was subsequently corrected, but errors of this nature are not uncommon, particularly in very large networks. Some of the smaller differences in location that were identified during the NE1 may have resulted from the difference between recently obtained global

positioning system (GPS) coordinates and coordinates that had been obtained manually from topographic maps, or differences in the horizontal datum used.

Well identification and location problems can be addressed by:

- labeling the well as specified by the FDEP;

- ensuring that all the well construction and location information is properly recorded and stored when a new well is being installed;

- creating detailed site maps that show the location of each well relative to several nearby permanent structures;

- collecting GPS coordinates and recording the datum to which the GPS is set. Differences between horizontal datums, such as North American Datum of 1983 and North American Datum of 1927, can be large enough in some areas to prevent technicians from finding wells; and

- ensuring that each well in a well nest is clearly identified and depths documented. A well nest is a group of wells that are clustered at one location, but open to an aquifer, or aquifers, at different depths.

The FDEP established the Florida Unique Well Identification (FLUWID) program to simplify the identification and exchange of well information between State agencies and interested parties. Under this program, each well is assigned a unique alphanumeric code that is printed on a weather resistant adhesive label that is attached to the well casing (Florida Department of Environmental Protection, 2008a). Alternatively, a metal tag or a brass disk can be stamped with the well information and attached directly to the protective casing of the well or embedded in the cement well pad. Paint or decals could be used to label a well but they would likely wear off through time, and in south Florida decals or stickers that are continuously exposed to the sun tend to become bleached out. Borehole camera examinations and well depth measurements can aid in identifying wells.

## Missing Well Construction Information

Well open intervals were not listed for 25 wells of the SFWMD-SWIMM network, 49 wells of the CCPCPD network, 213 wells of the inactive USGS-COOP-SWIM network, and 2 wells of the active USGS-COOP-SWIM network. If well depths or open intervals of wells are unknown, it is difficult to evaluate the quality of data being provided. If the well depth is unknown, for example, it is not possible to compute the proper purge volume. If the open interval is unknown, it may not be possible for a technician to determine the most appropriate sampling technique.

Some well construction information may be obtained during field inspections. The above-ground part of the well casing can be examined to confirm casing diameter and material. In some instances, however, this information may not represent the well construction below ground. For example, some old large-diameter black iron wells in south Florida have smaller diameter PVC casings installed and cemented into place within the large-diameter casing. So even though the well may appear to be cased with 2-inch-diameter PVC, this information may not be fully representative of the construction of the well. Borehole camera examinations and well depth measurements can be used to obtain some of the information that is missing.

In some instances, additional well construction records may be available through municipal, State, or Federal organizations. Much of the well construction information may exist in internal databases and documents at individual organizations in the JSWIM network. Some of these organizations have recorded much of the well construction and location information in relational, spatial databases or spreadsheets that can be queried by location, aquifer, well depth, or other properties of the well.

The JSWIM network could be improved by obtaining well construction information for existing wells, and better documentation of well construction information when new wells are added to the network. Well information folders can be created and organized for each new monitoring site. These folders can include (1) well location and construction information provided by the driller or others, (2) detailed sites maps with measured distances from the well to permanent objects, (3) street maps showing the general location of the site, (4) copies of lithologic or geophysical logs collected during installation, (5) permits or property access documents, (6) copies of survey notes (unless filed elsewhere), and (7) papers documenting well repairs.

## Wells That Were Not Designed to Provide Optimum Salinity Sampling or Monitoring

Monitoring of active public or private water-supply wells is important, but these wells cannot provide all the information needed to evaluate saltwater intrusion. The JSWIM network can be improved by installing new wells specifically designed, located, and monitored to evaluate saltwater intrusion and differentiate between the various sources of saltwater in the aquifers of the Big Cypress Basin.

## Damaged or Obstructed Monitoring Wells

Damaged or obstructed well casings can prevent accurate and precise measurements of salinity in the aquifer (fig. 8A). Wells with damaged casings may allow saltwater to mix with freshwater from above the saltwater interface. Wells with obstructed casings may prevent sampling equipment from being lowered to the necessary depth. Some wells in south Florida become filled with fine sand that flows up into the

well casing under hydrostatic pressure. In many instances, the USGS has used air lifting to clear the sediment from wells, but frequently the sediment flows back into the well casing to the same depth that it had previously filled the well. This sand may be transmissive enough to allow sampling of the well, but it may also make it difficult to determine whether the well is merely filled with sediment or if the casing has ruptured or separated. Thus, even if samples can be collected from these wells, there is no assurance that these samples are indicative of salinity in the aquifer at the depth of the well's designed open interval. Wells are better suited for long-term monitoring if filter packs and screens can be installed that prevent the fine sand from flowing into the well.

If a well is clogged, it may be difficult to distinguish between a damaged or obstructed well and a less transmissive aquifer or a confining unit. The FDEP indicates, therefore, that "immediately following well development, estimates of hydraulic conductivity can be obtained by conducting specific capacity tests" (Florida Department of Environmental Protection, 2008b, p. 49). This helps to establish a baseline condition to which subsequent measurements can be compared. FDEP Standard Operating Procedure FS2200 describes the need for water-level measurements prior to and during purging to ensure that water levels have stabilized, and that if a well "does not sustain pumping rates of at least 0.5 gallons per minute without excessive drawdown, other aquifer tests, such as slug tests should be performed" (Florida Department of Environmental Protection, 2008b, p. 49). The FDEP provides instructions for conducting these tests (Florida Department of Environmental Protection, 2008a, appendix C). Information concerning slug tests is available from ASTM International, (1996a, b), the California Environmental Protection Agency (1995), and the USGS (Halford and Kuniansky, 2002; U.S. Geological Survey, 2012e).

Some of the wells currently being monitored are damaged. For example the USGS has discontinued monitoring of some wells because damage or obstructions in wells could not be corrected using available resources, but a few of these wells, such as well C-977, are currently being monitored by other organizations. Many wells monitored by the USGS are owned by other organizations, these wells may still be monitored at the discretion of those organizations. Communication between organizations concerning well integrity could improve the quality of the JSWIM network.

One of the simplest improvements that could be made to the existing network is to periodically evaluate all existing wells to detect any problems that may prohibit the collection of samples that are representative of salinity in the aquifer at the well's designed open interval. Methods of evaluation could include total well-depth measurements, slug tests, pump tests, borehole video examinations, hydrographic comparison, geochemical sampling, and geophysical logging. Documentation of known well condition problems helps to ensure that these problems are addressed.

## Annual Well Depth Checks

Measured and recorded on an annual basis, the total well depth can provide a periodic check on well integrity and may help to verify well identification. Many of the monitoring wells in southwest Florida are installed in nests consisting of two or more wells that are open to different depths of an aquifer, or aquifers. Well depth measurements can be used to help distinguish between wells in these nests. If the measurement differs from the documented well construction or from previous measurements, further examinations may determine if (1) the correct well is being sampled, (2) the well construction documentation is correct, (3) the well casing has separated or is broken, (4) the well was reconstructed, or (5) the well is obstructed by sediment or foreign objects.

## Borehole Camera Inspections of Obstructed or Damaged Wells

Where the open interval of a well is unknown or where an annual well depth check indicates a difference between the listed depth and actual depth, a borehole camera examination can provide the information needed to evaluate these discrepancies. Borehole camera inspections have been used to identify problems that include (1) incorrect information in well construction records, (2) separated, broken, or corroded well casings, (3) collapsed sections of unscreened boreholes, (4) sampling devices that have become lodged in the well, (5) wells that have been reconstructed without proper documentation, and (5) screened or cased well segments that have become filled with debris. The information provided by these examinations makes it possible to determine whether a well can be rehabilitated or must be abandoned.

Old wells can potentially be added to a network if borehole camera logs can verify and document that the well construction and condition meet network requirements. Some organizations have conducted borehole camera examinations on all of their monitoring wells. Considering the expenditure of resources required for long-term monitoring, early identification of well construction or condition issues could be beneficial to the quality and efficiency of the JSWIM network.

## Abandonment of Wells that could Allow Aquifer Contamination

Wells that could allow aquifer contamination or wells that are not considered useful because of problems with their condition or integrity should be properly abandoned by following guidelines provided by the FDEP (2008a, p. 56). Test borings drilled to locate the saltwater interface are required to be abandoned by FDEP guidelines unless they are completed as monitoring wells that will be used for future tracking of the saltwater interface (Florida Department of Environmental Protection, 2008a). It is helpful to evaluate the network on a routine basis to identify wells that should be abandoned, ensure they are abandoned on a timely basis, and prevent a back log of wells requiring abandonment.

## Sampling Methodologies

Salinity monitoring methods used in south Florida include: (1) collection and analysis of groundwater samples using high volume or low volume suction pumps, submersible pumps, thief samplers, double valve bailers, or kemmerers, (2) continuous conductivity monitoring using a conductivity probe and internal or external data logger, and (3) water conductivity profiling using manual measurements or water-quality logging devices.

## Sample Collection Using Pumps

Variable speed centrifugal or peristaltic suction pumps are some of the easiest devices that can be used to collect water samples from a well. Suction pumps have an absolute theoretical limit of 34 ft of fresh head differential. Submersible pumps can be used where the head differential is greater than this, because they push water up an intake line rather than drawing it up by suction. Most of these pumps still have a maximum operating head differential, but generally this differential is not exceeded in south Florida.

The FDEP (2008b, p. 9) specifies that three consecutive measurements of temperature, pH, specific conductance, dissolved oxygen, and turbidity must fall within a specified range to ensure that stagnant water has been completely purged from monitoring wells. Other requirements such as stabilization of water level and amount of water purged are based on well design (2008b, p. 8). The USGS typically removes three to five well volumes of water prior to collecting water-quality samples from a well. The USGS measures stabilization parameters for some but not the majority of water samples for evaluation of chloride concentration or specific conductance.

The FDEP stipulates that "a variable speed centrifugal pump can be used to purge groundwater from 2-inch and larger internal diameter wells" but they state: "do not use this type of pump to collect groundwater samples" (2008b, section FS 2201, p. 2). Many of the organizations that collect salinity data follow this restriction. Although the USGS uses submersible pumps for some types of water-quality monitoring, variable-speed centrifugal pumps have been used for many years in south Florida to collect the majority of samples for analysis of chloride concentration and specific conductance. The procedures of the USGS differ from the FDEP FS2201 (2008b, p. 2); consequently, comparison of these two methods for the purposes of salinity monitoring would be helpful.

A limited survey of sampling procedures conducted during this study found that prior to sampling some of the monitoring wells were purged for 5 minutes using a peristaltic pump, at a rate of 4.5 gallons per minute (gal/min) to remove 22.5 gallons of water. The inlet hose of the pump was placed 2 ft below the water surface. The volume of the water column of these wells ranges from 9 to 30 gallons. The FDEP (2008b, p. 8–11) specifies that the amount of water purged prior to sampling should be based on well design, the volume of water in the well, and monitoring of stabilization parameters, rather than pumping for set period of time. The FDEP (2008b, p. 8–11) requires that at least one well volume must be purged prior to collection of stabilization parameters, three consecutive measurements of the stabilization parameters must be within the stated limits, and that at least one quarter of a well volume must be purged between subsequent measurements. The 22.5 gallons removed prior to sampling, therefore, is insufficient in some instances because the minimum purge volume ranges from 13.5 to 45 gallons for these wells. Additional purging may also be needed before the stabilization parameters are within required limits. Some of these samples, therefore, may not be representative of the water in the aquifer at the well's screened interval. An expanded survey of sampling procedures used for the JSWIM program is considered to be an important tool to better understand the quality of information that can be obtained through this network. Direct observation of sampling procedures being used would be even more informative.

## Improved Sampling Guidelines

If applied without modification, the sampling guidelines established by the FDEP (Florida Department of Environmental Protection, 2008b) may include some samples that are not representative of the maximum salinity in the aquifer at the open depth well interval. FDEP standard operating procedures (SOPs) for groundwater sampling (Florida Department of Environmental Protection, 2008b) divides wells into two main categories: (1) wells without plumbing (typically monitoring wells sampled with portable pumps); and (2) wells with in-place plumbing, such as water-supply wells typically found in well fields, industrial facilities, and private residences that have fixed pumps. Section FS2213 of these SOPs describes purging of wells without plumbing and specifies: "Do not lower pump or intake hose (tubing) to the bottom of the well. Pump or tubing placement procedures will be determined by the purging option selected..." This section also specifies that if the following conditions are met, the pump intake hose should be positioned in the screened or open borehole interval.

- The same pump is used for both purging and sampling.

- The well screen or borehole interval must be less than or equal to 10 ft.

- The well screen or borehole must be fully submerged.

Only 19 percent of the JSWIM network wells have documented open intervals of less than or equal to 10 ft. About 70 percent of the documented well have open intervals that are greater than or equal to 20 ft and about 30 percent have open intervals greater than or equal to 100 ft. The majority of the wells of the JSWIM network, therefore, have to be purged as described in sections FS 2213.1.2 or FS 2214 of the FDEP SOPs. Section FS 2213.1.2 entitled "Conventional Purging", specifies: "Position the pump or intake tubing in the top one foot of the water column or no deeper than necessary for the type of pump." Section FS 2214 entitled "Purging

Large-Volume, High-Recharge Wells with Portable Pumps" specifies that the well is purged by "placing the pump at the top of the open borehole segment of the well." Based on these sampling procedures, it appears that the majority of wells lacking in-place plumbing in the JSWIM network would be sampled with the pump or intake tubing placed near the top of the screen or the top of the water column. This type of sampling has been demonstrated to yield salinity samples that are not representative of maximum salinity in the aquifer in the depth interval to which the well is open.

Kohout and Hoy (1963) observed additional sampling difficulties associated with long open-interval wells. When a freshwater-saltwater interface occurs within the long open interval of a well, and the intake of the pump is placed above this interface, "water tends to come from the upper part of the open borehole because less energy is expended by removal of low-density water from this region than by removal of high-density water from the lower part of the open borehole."

Data collected by the USGS from many wells in southwest Florida show an increase in specific conductance with depth associated with the saltwater interface (fig. 9). In some of the examples provided, the maximum specific conductance occurs some distance above the bottom of the well, but in all of these examples the salinity at the bottom of the open interval is higher than near the top of the open interval.

Kohout and Hoy (1963) also determined that samples taken from long open intervals preferentially represent salinity of the most permeable strata rather than the depth of maximum salinity in the borehole, and that the amount of dilution within the well bore was variable as a result of hydrologic conditions. They concluded that the overall quality of data collected by this method was poor. Salinity data obtained from well L-5723 (fig. 10) provide an example of misinterpretation of the position of the saltwater interface caused by sampling long open-interval wells when using pumps that draw water from the upper part of the water column. Well L-5723 has an open interval from 55 to 140 ft bls and was sampled periodically from March 27, 1986, to March 9, 1999, by withdrawing water near the top of the water column with a suction pump. Specific conductance and chloride concentration sampled during this period averaged 877 microsiemens per centimeter ($\mu$S/cm) and 94 mg/L, respectively, and was not changing (fig. 10A). Specific conductance profiles collected from this well between November 1998 and May 2000 showed that a saltwater interface intersected the open interval of the well in the depth interval 85 to 100 ft bls and that the specific conductance near the bottom of the well was about 4,050 $\mu$S/cm (fig. 10B). During the period April 9, 1999, to April 21, 2004, this well was sampled by using a kemmerer sampler that was lowered to near the bottom of the well. Water samples indicated an average specific conductance and chloride concentration of 3,880 $\mu$S/cm and 890 mg/L, respectively. Application of an alternative sampling procedure resulted in nearly an order of magnitude change in the chloride concentration of samples. Data collected prior to April 9, 1999, could have led to an underestimate of the extent of saltwater intrusion at this

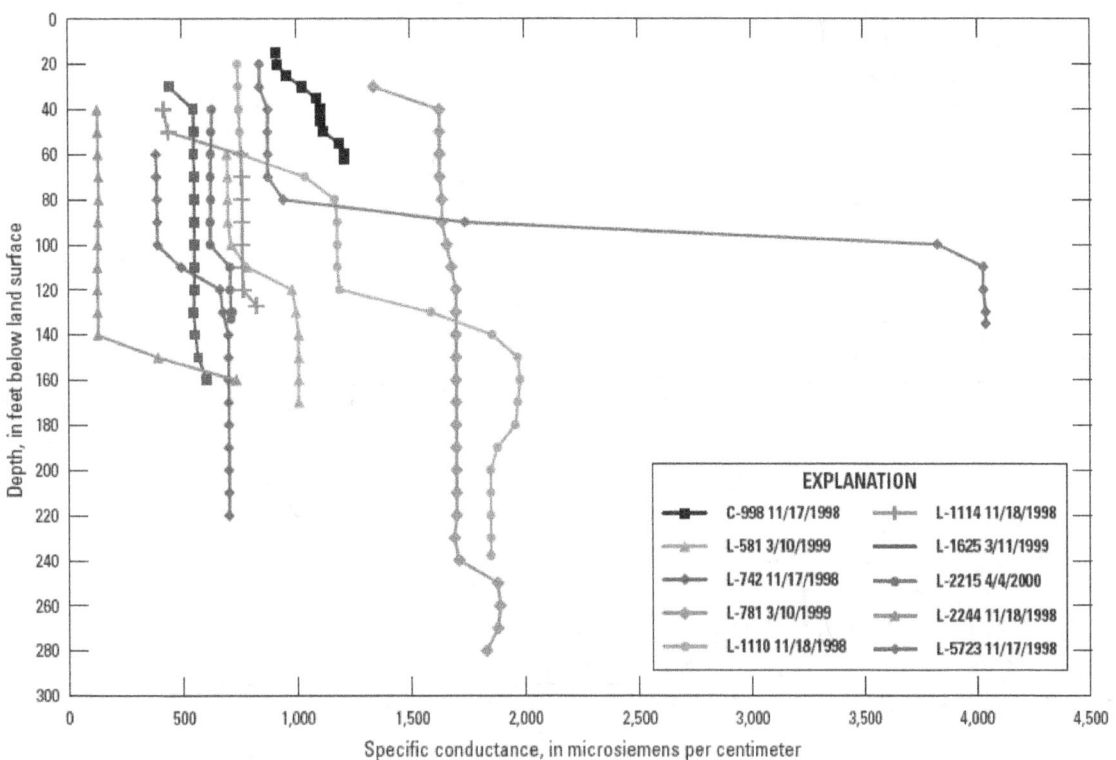

**Figure 9.**  Specific conductance profiles collected in selected long open-interval wells monitored by the U.S. Geological Survey in Lee and Collier Counties of southwest Florida.

location, leading to poor management decisions. These data could also have resulted in poor model calibrations.

Vertical flow within the well may also prevent collection of a sample representative of the maximum salinity. Geophysical and geochemical logging conducted at various locations in south Florida, and elsewhere reveals that ambient flow commonly occurs within the open bore of long-screened wells and that this flow has the potential to bias the results of water samples or conductivity profiles (Johnson and others, 2002; Shapiro, 2002; Oki and Presley, 2008; Runkel and others, 2008; Shalev and others, 2009). Oki and Presley (2008), for example, describe alterations of the saltwater interface induced by vertical flow in long open-interval wells in Hawaii. They demonstrated that a naturally occurring saltwater interface can be distorted in several ways. Divergent vertical well-bore flow at the same depth as the interface can thicken the interface within the well. Downward or upward vertical flow can also shift the depth of the interface in the water column of the well relative to that in the aquifer. Shalev and others (2009) collected continuous salinity records at depths of 62.0, 67.8, 73.4, 79.2, and 85.0 ft bls in a borehole near the coast in Tel-Aviv, Israel. Information collected quantified oscillations in the depth of the saltwater interface within a borehole resulting from tidal oscillations in aquifer water levels. Using a 3-dimensional

numerical model, they determined that fluctuations in the depth of the interface occurring within long open boreholes were an order of magnitude larger than those in the porous media of the aquifer. Shalev and others (2009) attribute this difference to the anisotropy and hydraulic conductivity of the aquifer, relative to the hydraulic conductivity of the borehole. Church and Granato (1996) compared induction logs and sample results from nests of short open-interval wells to the sample results from proximal (maximum spacing 32 ft) long open-interval wells. They found that even in a relatively homogeneous, unconfined sand and gravel aquifer, the sample results from the long screened wells were not fully representative of water quality in the aquifer.

Some of the long open-interval wells examined in the NE1 may penetrate confining units between aquifers (BEM Systems Inc., 2003), which could cause movement of saltwater between aquifers. An evaluation of hydrostratigraphy, water quality, and well-bore flow on a well-by-well basis would indicate where this is a problem.

In a report describing guidelines and standard procedures for studies of groundwater quality, Lapham and others (1997, p. 28) recommend wells with screen lengths of 5 ft or less for studies on the fate and transport of groundwater constituents for the following reasons:

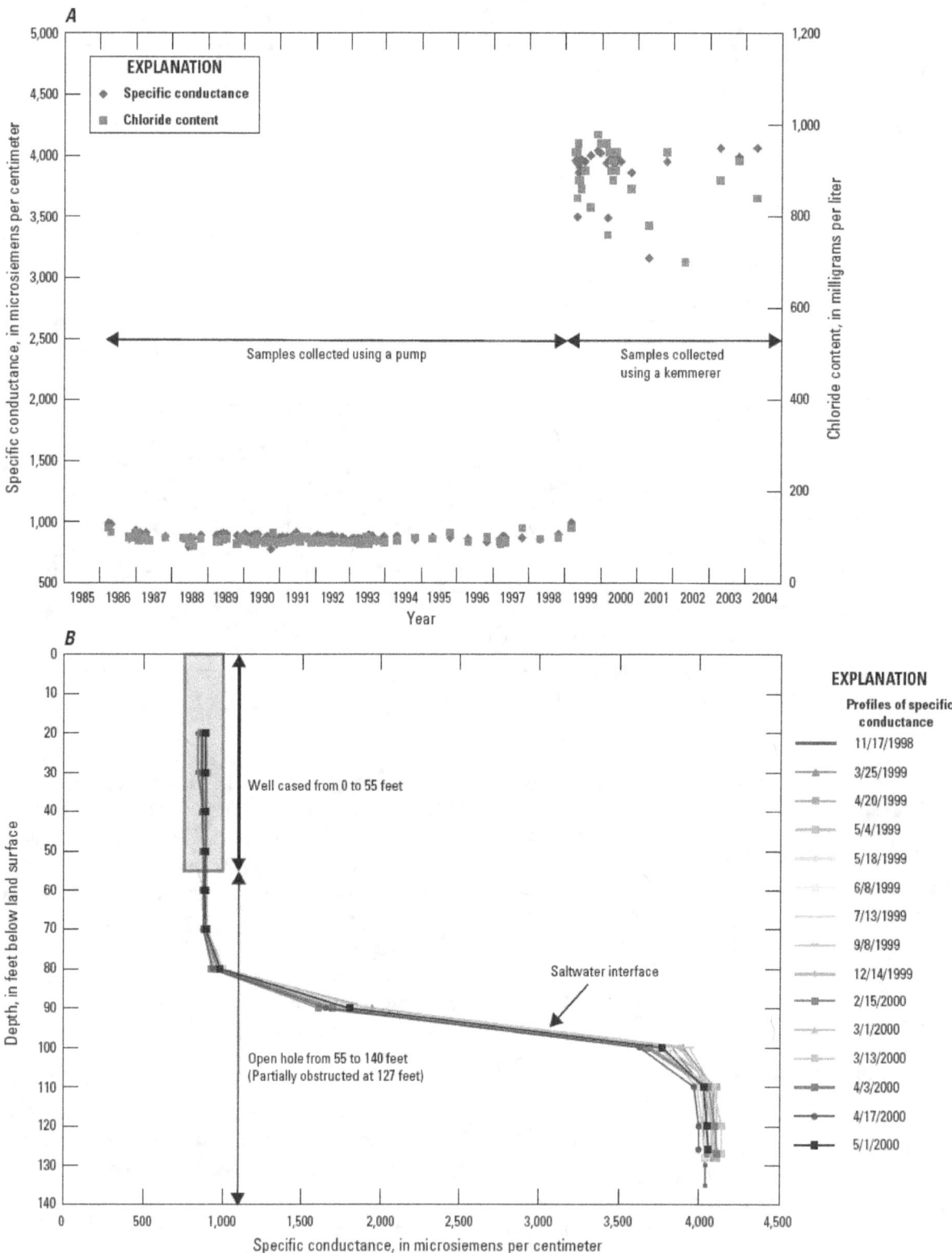

**Figure 10.**  Salinity at well L-5723 in Lee County, Florida, (*A*) chloride concentration and specific conductance of collected water samples, and (*B*) specific conductance profiles.

- A short-screened well generally provides measurements of hydraulic head and groundwater quality that more closely represent point measurements in the aquifer than measurements provided by a long screen.

- Samples obtained from wells with long screened intervals could exhibit smaller concentrations or a higher frequency of samples with nondetectable concentrations (leading to a 'false negative' assessment) in comparison to water samples from wells with short screened intervals (McIlvride and Rector, 1988).

- A long well screen also can induce mixing of waters of different chemistry as compared to a short well screen due to vertical groundwater flow and head differences in the screened interval (well-bore flow). Well-bore flow has been reported even in homogeneous aquifers with small vertical head differences (Reilly and others, 1989). Well-bore flow may contribute to aquifer contamination by providing a pathway for contaminant movement along the screened interval(s).

Improvements to the JSWIM network require development of a set of custom-designed SOPs for salinity sampling to which all organizations in the JSWIM network will adhere. Subsequent sections of this report will discuss additional sampling considerations that would be helpful to consider during development of SOPs. Where long open-interval wells are being used primarily for saltwater intrusion monitoring, the network can potentially be improved by quantifying the effects of mixing and vertical flow within the boreholes of these wells using borehole geophysical methods described in subsequent sections of this report. These examinations provide the most detailed information if conducted under varying hydrologic conditions. The JSWIM network could also be improved by installing new monitoring wells with 5-ft open intervals, screens, and filter packs.

In many instances, it will not be possible to improve the sampling protocols because many long open-interval wells being sampled are public or private water-supply wells with permanently installed pumps. While sampling helps ensure that the quality of water being withdrawn for public supply meets acceptable standards, sampling difficulties associated with long open-interval wells impairs accurate mapping, modeling, or monitoring of saltwater intrusion.

## Alternative Methods of Sampling Long-Open Interval Wells

There are several alternative methods for monitoring salinity change in long open-interval wells which may help to mitigate previously described problems. These include (1) micro-purging using a low speed pump that draws water from near the bottom of the well's open interval, (2) collection of samples using double check-valve bailers or kemmerers, (3) a combination of purging from near the water surface and collection of samples using a pump or sampler from the bottom of the well, and (4) conductivity profiling.

### Micro-Purging

Micro-purging consists of pumping a well with the intake of the pump located within the screened interval of a well to remove a minimum amount of water at flow rates of approximately 0.1 gal/min. Pumping at these rates theoretically withdraws water from along a single flow line (through the screen of the well) and does not induce negligible drawdown in the well. This method assumes that groundwater can flow freely through the open interval of a well. Kohout and Hoy (1963) described a similar method for purging a minimum volume of water from a well to collect a sample from the depth of maximum salinity. Various organizations have developed protocols for micro-purging (Indiana Department of Environmental Management, 1998; New Mexico Environment Department, 2001). Kearl and others (1994) showed that water from the aquifer that flowed through the screened interval during micro-purging did not mix with water in the casing of the well. This sampling technique may be used to provide representative samples of maximum salinity from some long open-interval wells in southwest Florida. For example, profiles of specific conductance collected in wells L-581, L-742, and L-1110 indicated that salinity was at a maximum and was relatively constant in the depth intervals of 130–170, 140–220, and 150–180 ft bls, respectively (fig. 9). Based on these thicknesses and the volumes or rates of water removed by micro-purging, it is unlikely that enough vertical flow would be created within the borehole to dilute the resulting samples from these wells.

The New Mexico Environment Department (2001) points out that "Micropurging does not have a mechanism to verify that the sample results are indicative of water quality in the formation surrounding the well. The water obtained has the potential to be stagnant…" In addition, samples may still be affected by ambient vertical flow within the borehole. The applicability of this sampling technique could be tested in the Big Cypress Basin.

### Discrete Depth Samplers

Discrete-depth sampling using nonisokinetic thief samplers was proposed as an alternative method of sampling salinity in long open-borehole wells in south Florida by Kohout and Hoy (1963). A number of nonisokinetic thief samplers are commercially available (Lane and others, 2003, p. 33–34), including double check-valve bailers and kemmerers. Currently the USGS is using kemmerers to collect samples from long open-interval wells in south Florida. Kemmerers are lowered on a line to the desired depth, and a weight called a messenger is sent down the line. The messenger triggers a mechanism on the top of the kemmerer that causes the stoppers on both ends of the sampler to snap shut and trap a sample in the bottle. The kemmerer can prematurely close, however, so care must be taken in lowering the sampler. It is also helpful to test a portion of the sample with a conductivity meter prior to departing from the site to ensure the sample is in reasonable agreement with the history of previous measurements. Nonisokinetic thief samplers can be used to collect a sample from near the bottom of the well's open interval, but care should be taken to avoid contacting the bottom of the well with the sampler because this could stir up sediments that adversely affect the sample and impair the seal of the sampler.

The FDEP (2008b, p. 34) describes the use of bailers for sampling. The FDEP recommends that if bailers are used that they be constructed with dual check valves and that they not be used for purging (2008b, p. 34–35). The FDEP specifies that it is necessary to "Lower and retrieve the bailer slowly and smoothly" (Florida Department of Environmental Protection, 2008b, p. 16). Disposable bailers can be advantageous because they prevent cross contamination between wells and are recommended by the FDEP for sampling grossly contaminated sample sources (Florida Department of Environmental Protection, 2008b, p. 4). Like mirco-purging, there is no way to verify that sample results are indicative of water quality in an aquifer, and vertical well-bore flow could potentially affect samples.

### Sampling Using a Combination of Techniques

A disadvantage of using discrete depth samplers is that they do not draw water from the aquifer into the well to clear out any stagnant water. This disadvantage could be overcome by purging the well using a suction pump with a shallow intake line prior to sampling with a discrete depth sampler. One potential problem with this method is that when purging is completed, the salinity may continue to decrease after purging (Kohout and Hoy, 1963).

Another technique is to use two pumps to collect the sample. One pump with its intake near the surface could be used for purging and maintaining an upward flow in the well, while a second pump with its intake located near the bottom of the long open interval could be used to collect the sample. This method of sampling removes stagnant water from the well while also ensuring upward flow within the borehole. The highest salinity usually occurs at the bottom of the well, because saltwater is denser than freshwater; however, this may not be true in every instance (fig. 9).

### Specific Conductance

Specific conductance measurements can be used to evaluate salinity. Specific conductance can be measured in a discrete water sample, or vertically along a borehole using a submersible probe. Conductivity profiles are much easier to collect than a series of discrete-depth sampler profiles. Some of the submersible probes being used can collect a large number of individual measurements in a short period of time. Some probes can collect a data point every tenth of a foot or less. The data provided by these profiles are less ambiguous than results from groundwater samples collected using suction pumps in long open-interval wells because the amount of mixing of freshwater and saltwater induced by passage of the probe is minimal. Specific conductance profiles of long open-interval wells like those shown in figures 9 and 10*B* have been used to measure changes in the depth to the top of the

saltwater interface and changes in the salinity of water in the well. There is, however, still the potential for uncertainty in these data because water conductivity profiles can be affected by ambient vertical flow in the borehole.

## Distinguishing Sources of Saline Groundwater

Determining the source of salinity (fig. 6) may allow various distinctions, such as the differentiation between encroaching saltwater that threatens the viability of a well field, and residual saltwater that is dissipating. Making those distinctions could require the collection of additional types of water-quality data. Some of these types of data have already been collected in south Florida and proven to be useful. These types of data include (1) strontium-87/strontium-86 ratio (Schmerge, 2001), (2) oxygen and hydrogen stable isotopes (Schmerge, 2001), (3) tritium-helium age dating (Schlosser and others, 1988), and (4) major and trace ion geochemistry (Richter and Kreitler, 1993, p. 103–107). Schmerge (2001) used the strontium-87/strontium-86 ratio of water samples from the aquifers of southwest Florida to evaluate the age of aquifer materials with which groundwater had equilibrated. His results indicated that groundwater from some deep aquifers leaked upward to intrude portions of shallower aquifers. Schmerge (2001) has shown that the oxygen and hydrogen stable isotopic signature of meteoric water in southwest Florida is different than that of seawater or water from deeper confined aquifers. This understanding can be used and expanded upon to differentiate between the sources of saltwater in the aquifer. Richter and Kreitler (1993, p. 103–107) describe some of the changes in major and trace ion geochemistry that typically occur as seawater mixes with freshwater in a coastal aquifer. This mixing takes place in a transition zone near the leading edge of the front. Where saltwater is intruding into previously fresh portions of the aquifer, chemical reactions with aquifer materials change the composition of the water relative to that created solely by mechanical mixing. These changes in composition allow scientists to differentiate between an actively advancing saltwater front and saltwater that occurs in previously intruded parts of the aquifer.

## Relation of the Network to the Hydrostratigraphic Framework

Evaluation of saltwater intrusion in an aquifer requires a clear understanding of the depths from which salinity samples emanate relative to the base of the aquifer. Saltwater is denser than freshwater and tends to settle to the base of an aquifer. It is important, therefore, to clearly understand the hydrostratigraphy of the aquifer and the aquifer units that the open interval of a well penetrates. The NE1 found that there are substantial differences in aquifer depths and thicknesses depicted in the BEM Systems Inc. (2003) interpretation compared with the hydrostratigraphic interpretations of Wedderburn and others (1982) and Knapp and others (1986). These differences have led to differences in the aquifer assignments of wells. These differences need to be resolved before the data from these wells can be used to evaluate saltwater intrusion.

The dataset compiled by BEM Systems Inc. (2003) included data collected and recorded by various organizations. Concerning this issue, BEM System Inc. (2003, p. 5) noted that some of those data may be erroneous. They used statistical checks and geostatistical analyses to identify possible outliers. But they did not re-interpret the hydrostratigraphic interpretations of information from individual test wells. This could potentially lead to inconsistencies because there is disagreement concerning the hydrostratigraphy of southwest Florida. For example, Edwards and others (1998, p. 10) indicate that the siliciclastics near the base of the Tamiami Formation have been interpreted to be within "the Miocene Coarse Clastics, Hawthorn Group, and lower Tamiami Formation (Knapp and others, 1986; Smith and Adams, 1988), within the Tamiami Formation (Peck and others, 1979), or entirely within the Hawthorn Group (Peacock, 1983; Campbell, 1988; Missimer, 1997). Green and others (1990), referred to these sediments as 'undifferentiated coarse siliciclastics' and suggested that the sediments were, at least in part Pliocene." An important question is whether merging of hydrostratigraphic interpretations by various organizations over a broad period of time, affects the final interpretation developed by BEM Systems Inc. (2003). Prior to reassignment of wells to different aquifers, existing or newly collected hydrostratigraphic information could be used to evaluate this issue.

High quality hydrostratigraphic interpretations can be obtained using a combination of coring, aquifer testing, and geophysical logging including: borehole image, caliper, electromagnetic induction, flow, full waveform sonic, gamma, single point resistance, spontaneous potential and water-quality logs. Yet many of the existing hydrostratigraphic interpretations available from southwest Florida were based on less comprehensive geophysical and stratigraphic information. Cuttings are frequently used rather than core. It is often difficult to use cuttings alone to determine if a particular stratum is hydraulically conductive. If a geospatial analysis used to interpret hydrostratigraphic information does not consider the differences in quality of the information available, it may be unduly influenced by poor quality yet more plentiful data. Prior to re-classification of wells by aquifer, it is important to understand the differences in stratigraphic interpretation and variations in the quality of data on which these interpretations are based. In some instances, additional geophysical logging, water-quality sampling, and aquifer testing can be collected to aid in this evaluation.

Previous hydrostratigraphic interpretations were generally presented as a series of contour lines on maps. The BEM Systems Inc. (2003) interpretation has been represented as a series of gridded surfaces that can be loaded into a GIS, which made it easier to compare well data to the hydrostratigraphic framework. The contours had one advantage; however, where data were insufficient for mapping, the contour lines could be dashed. These dashed lines helped to indicate where additional

stratigraphic information was needed. If possible it would be beneficial to provide similar indications of data sufficiency for the GIS surfaces created by BEM Systems Inc. (2003).

## Spatial Coverage of the Saltwater Intrusion Monitoring Network

The JSWIM network is dense in some areas and sparse in others. Ideally, monitoring wells would be located to tightly bracket the leading edge of the saltwater front where saltwater has encroached laterally from the Gulf, so that the front movement could be quantified. Spatial coverage of the JSWIM network can be improved by (1) collecting additional surface-water data upstream from salinity control structures, (2) installing new monitoring wells where necessary to bracket the saltwater front and areas of leakage between aquifers, and (3) collecting of surface or airborne geophysical measurements.

### Salinity of Surface-Water Bodies

The spatial coverage of the JSWIM network can be improved by considering where saltwater is flowing, or might flow inland up rivers or canals to intrude the surficial aquifer. Salinity control structures have been installed in most of the canals of southwest Florida to try to mitigate saltwater intrusion. Leach and Grantham (1966, p. 25) and Parker and others (1955), however, have documented the occurrence of saltwater upstream from salinity control structures in south Florida. If saltwater is present upstream of a salinity control structure in the Big Cypress Basin, when the structure is closed and the freshwater head on the upstream side of the structure increases, this saltwater can driven out into the aquifer by the hydrologic gradient (Kohout and Leach, 1964). The specific conductance of surface water in southwest Florida is being monitored by the CCPCPD and the LCNRD (tables 2-2, 2-6). The monitoring conducted by the CCPCPD has detected saltwater at 7 of the sites that are located between the salinity control structures closest to the coast and the next structures upstream. At four of the seven sites, BC7, BC8, BC22, and FAKA (figs. 11 and 11A), during January 2007 - December 2008, 8 to 19 percent of the measurements of specific conductance were in excess of 3,000 µS/cm, which is approximately equivalent to a chloride concentration of 1,000 mg/L. Most measurements that exceeded a specific conductance value of 3,000 µS/cm were salinity samples collected between April and July 2007 and in May 2008. This finding indicates that saltwater may be leaking past the water-control structures during the dry season when freshwater runoff is limited and canal stage and groundwater levels on the landward side of salinity control structures are low.

The Gordon River is located on the eastern side of the city of Naples Coastal Ridge well field (fig. 11B). Measurements of specific conductance at site BC-3 on the Gordon River, 0.7 mi downstream from structure GORDON (fig. 11B), indicate a mean specific conductance of 23,882 µS/cm

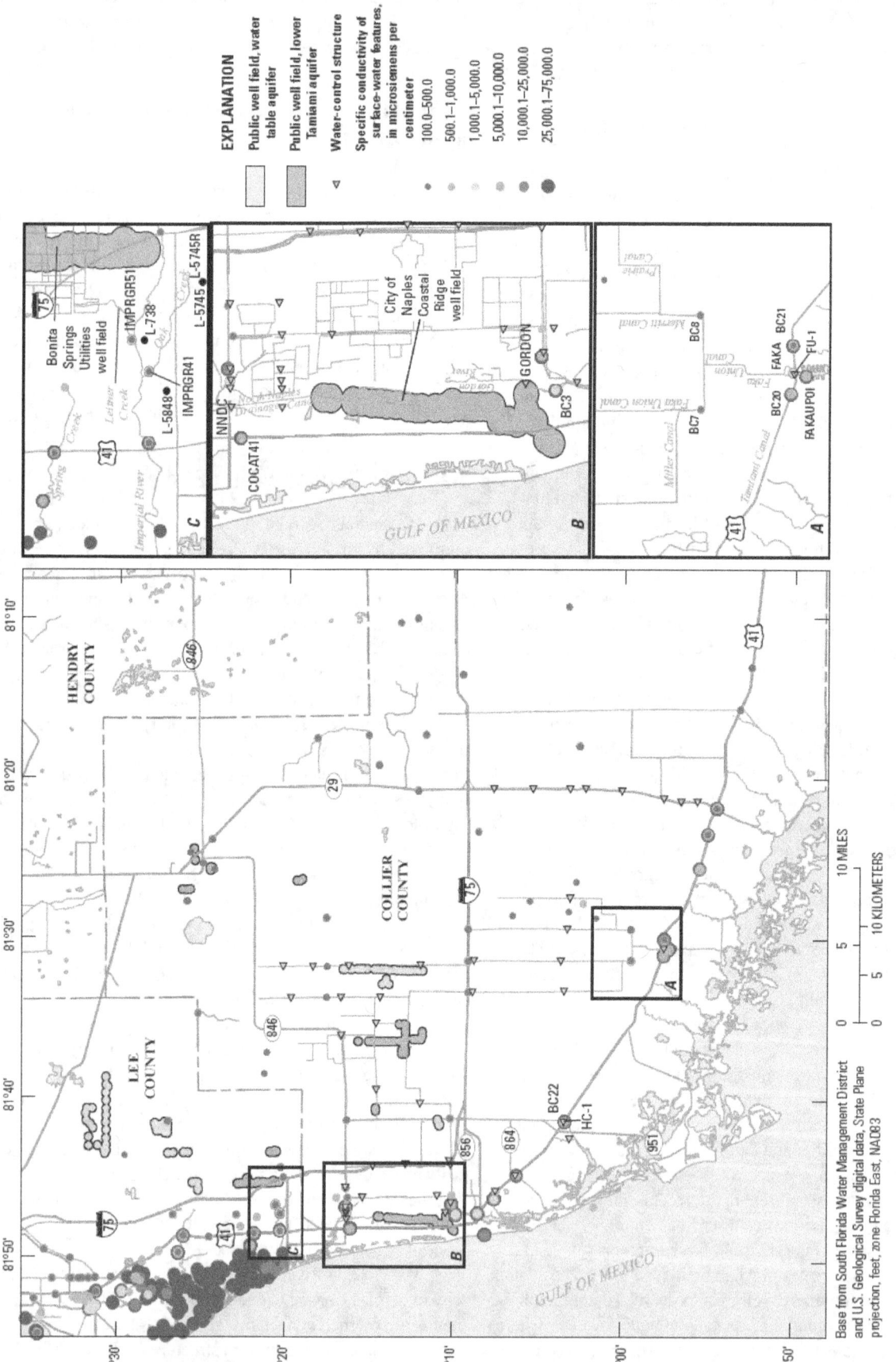

**Figure 11.** Salinity of surface-water bodies in Lee and Collier Counties, southwest Florida, 2007–2008. Inset maps *A*, *B*, and *C*, provide greater detail for selected areas.

Base from South Florida Water Management District and U.S. Geological Survey digital data, State Plane projection, feet, zone Florida East, NAD83

EXPLANATION

Public well field, water table aquifer

Public well field, lower Tamiami aquifer

Water-control structure

Specific conductivity of surface-water features, in microsiemens per centimeter

100.0–500.0
500.1–1,000.0
1,000.1–5,000.0
5,000.1–10,000.0
10,000.1–25,000.0
25,000.1–75,000.0

during 2007–2008. Some of this saltwater may be leaking into the surficial aquifer system in this area. No salinity samples were collected from the Gordon River upstream from structure GORDON (fig. 11*B*). The North Naples Drainage Canal extends from the Cocohatchee River (fig. 1) south to the city of Naples Coastal Ridge well field (fig. 11*B*). Salinity control structure NNDC (fig. 11*B*) may prevent saltwater from flowing down this canal, but salinity samples were not collected upstream from structure NNDC in 2007 and 2008 to verify this assumption.

Just north of the Big Cypress Basin, in Bonita Springs, water with a specific conductance as high as 37,100 μS/cm was detected 2.8 mi inland along the Imperial River (fig. 11*C*, table 2-6). In two tributaries of the Imperial River, Oak Creek and Leitner Creek, water samples were collected from measuring sites IMPRGR41 and IMPRGR51 located 4.0 and 4.5 mi inland, respectively. Maximum specific conductance of samples collected during the period 2007–2008 was 23,200 μS/cm at site IMPRGR41 in Oak Creek and 14,500 μS/cm at site IMPRGR51in Leitner Creek. The westernmost wells of the Bonita Springs Utilities well field are only 1.5 mi farther east of these two sampling locations (fig. 11*C*), and it is possible that salinity could increase during prolonged drought periods. Leakage of saltwater from these rivers could also contribute to elevated salinity of water samples collected from monitoring wells L-738, L-5745, L-5745R, and L-5848, all of which are located within 0.5 mi of the Imperial River or its tributaries.

The JSWIM network could be improved by collecting samples upstream of salinity control structures near the Gordon River and North Naples Drainage Canal to verify that saltwater is not leaking past these structures. If leakage is detected, monitoring wells could be installed between these surface-water bodies and the city of Naples Coastal Ridge well field. If saltwater is periodically detected upstream of the salinity control structures, continuous salinity monitoring provides better information than periodic sampling for evaluating potential influxes of saltwater in the canals and into the aquifer. A time series of electromagnetic induction logs can be collected from wells adjacent to the river to assess the intrusion of saline surface water into the aquifer.

## Water-Table Aquifer

The principal water-table aquifer well fields in the Big Cypress Basin are the Golden Gate Water Treatment Facility and the city of Naples East Golden Gate well field, located 7 mi and 17 to 18 mi inland from the coast, respectively (fig. 12). According to the interpretation of BEM Systems Inc. (2003), the top of the Bonita Springs marl member (the base of the water-table aquifer) at the Golden Gate Water Treatment Facility and city of Naples East Golden Gate well field is 24 to 27 ft bls and 13 to 27 ft bls, respectively. Most Golden Gate Water Treatment Facility wells are open in the depth interval 15 to 22 ft bls. Two public water-supply wells, GG-3 and GG-4, are open in the depth interval 35 to 45 ft bls, which according to the hydrostratigraphic interpretation

of BEM Systems Inc. (2003) would be in the lower Tamiami aquifer rather than the water-table aquifer. Monitoring wells MW-B (45 ft deep), MW-C (65 ft deep), MW-D (101 ft deep), and MW-F (60 ft deep) near the Golden Gate Water Treatment Facility (fig. 12) are also listed as being open to the water-table aquifer but would actually be open to the lower Tamiami aquifer.

Many of the wells that are currently being sampled between the Gulf of Mexico, the Golden Gate Water Treatment Facility, and the city of Naples East Golden Gate well field, fully penetrate the water-table aquifer and yield freshwater. These wells should provide ample warning of saltwater encroachment along the base of the water-table aquifer from the Gulf of Mexico. The majority of these wells were sampled by the CCPCPD in 2007. Almost all of the samples from wells east of U.S. Highway 41 indicated chloride concentrations of less than 250 mg/L. Exceptions were well CCS3 located on State Highway 84 about 2 mi east of U.S. Highway 41 and well CCN4 located 1.9 mi east of U.S. Highway 41 and 0.7 north of Immokalee Road (fig. 12). The samples from these wells had chloride concentrations of 281 and 327 mg/L, respectively.

Median water-level altitudes from wells C-951, C-953, C-976, C-977, C-985, C-988, and C-1097 (fig. 12), completed in the water-table and lower Tamiami aquifers near the Golden Gate Water Treatment Facility and the city of Naples East Golden Gate well field, were between 6 and 11 ft. The Ghyben-Herzberg principle (Ghyben, 1889; Herzberg, 1901) indicates that these water levels under hydrostatic conditions should be sufficient to prevent saltwater from encroaching inland to the well fields. This does not mean that these well fields cannot be affected by saltwater intrusion but rather that the saltwater encroaching inland from the Gulf of Mexico is unlikely to reach the well fields.

The maximum chloride concentration sampled from monitoring wells MW-C and MW-D during 2007 was 380 and 3,600 mg/L, respectively. Chloride concentration has increased gradually in wells C-953 (40 ft deep), located 3 mi west of the city of Naples East Golden Gate well field, and C-1061(25 ft deep), in Naples near the west coast (figs. 1, 3, 12). Between the late 1980s and 2011, the average chloride concentration in wells C-953 and C-1061 increased by approximately 35 and 85 mg/L, respectively. The high chloride concentration sampled in monitoring well MW-D and the increasing chloride concentration in monitoring well C-953 may have resulted from the movement of residual seawater or water that has leaked upward from deeper aquifers. Well C-1061 is much closer to the coast; therefore, the increase in chloride concentration at this location could be caused by saltwater encroaching from the Gulf of Mexico.

The wells sampled by CCPCPD in April and May 2009 are not shown on the SFWMD map of the 250 mg/L isochlor in Collier County in April and May 2009 (South Florida Water Management District, 2011b) (Appendix 1, fig. 1-2). Inclusion of these data could improve updates of these maps. CCPCPD sampling of wells MW-5, MW-10, and MW-11 located west

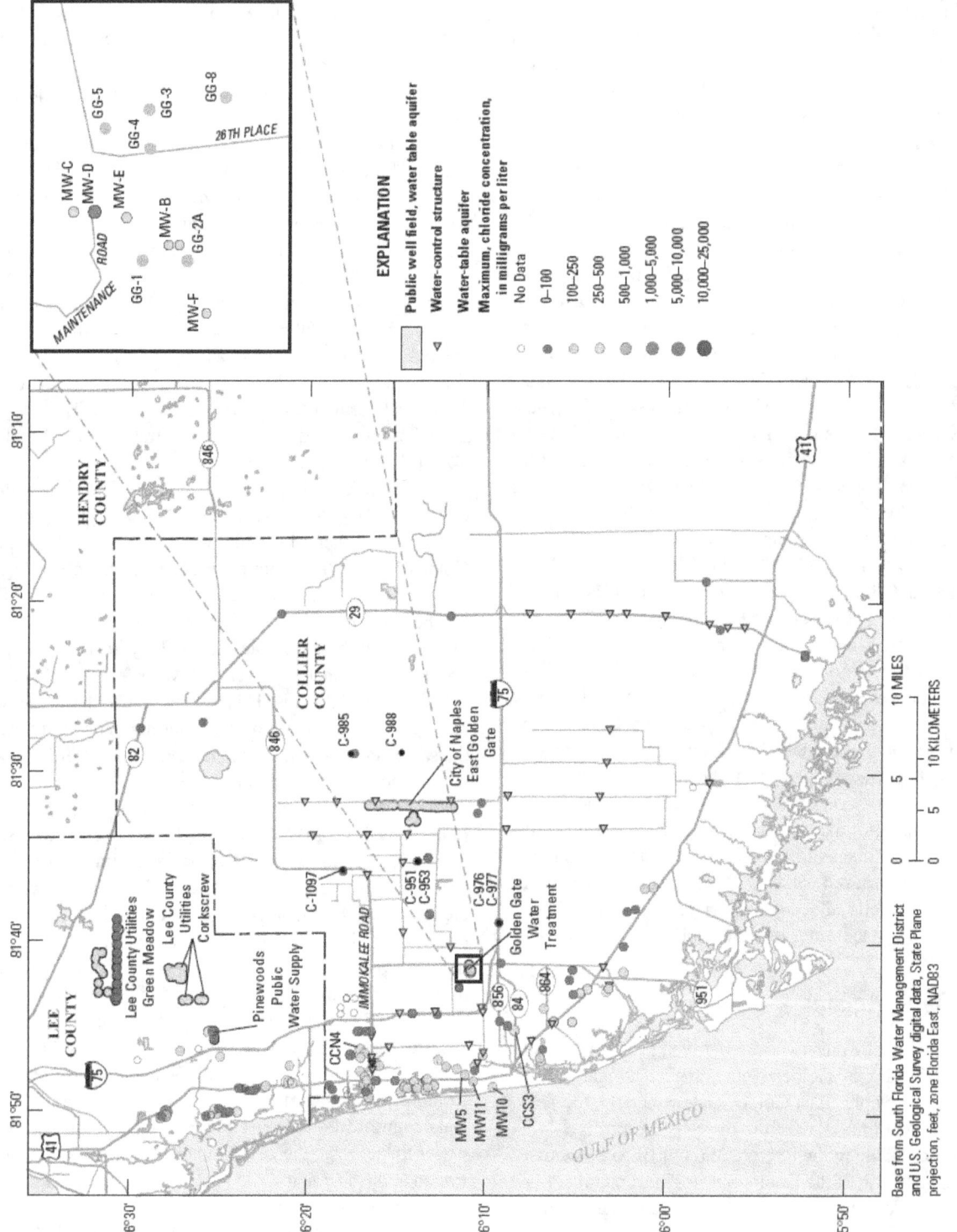

**Figure 12.**   Location of public water-supply wells and the maximum concentration of chloride in samples collected from monitoring wells open to the water-table aquifer.

of the Gordon River and Naples Bay and well CCN4 located near the Cocohatchee River and 3.7 mi from the coast could potentially be coordinated with the data collection for mapping of the 250 mg/L isochlor.

## Lower Tamiami Aquifer

In 2007 withdrawals from the lower Tamiami aquifer were reported from the Ave Maria Utility Company well field, Bonita Springs Utilities well field, the city of Naples Coastal Ridge well field, the Citrus Park RV Resort well field, the Collier County Utilities Golden Gate and North Hawthorn well fields, and the Immokalee Water and Sewer District Carlson Road, Airport Plant, and Jerry V. Warden well fields (fig. 13). The NE1 found that 47 percent of the 252 wells being monitored for the SFWMD-SWIMM network in the lower Tamiami

aquifer are either public water-supply wells or are within 100 ft of the public water-supply. Many of the remaining wells in the SFWMD-SWIMM network are other water-supply wells such as irrigation wells.

Well LT-1A is the only well of the LCNRD network open to the lower Tamiami aquifer. Of the 12 CCPCPD monitoring network wells open to the lower Tamiami aquifer, five are discontinued USGS-COOP-SWIM network monitoring wells. All but one of the CCPCPD wells are located farther inland than the city of Naples Coastal Ridge well field. The USGS currently (2012) monitors salinity at 10 wells in the lower Tamiami aquifer. Most of these are located between the coast and the city of Bonita Springs and city of Naples Coastal Ridge well fields. Of these 10 wells, chloride concentration has been gradually increasing in 6 wells.

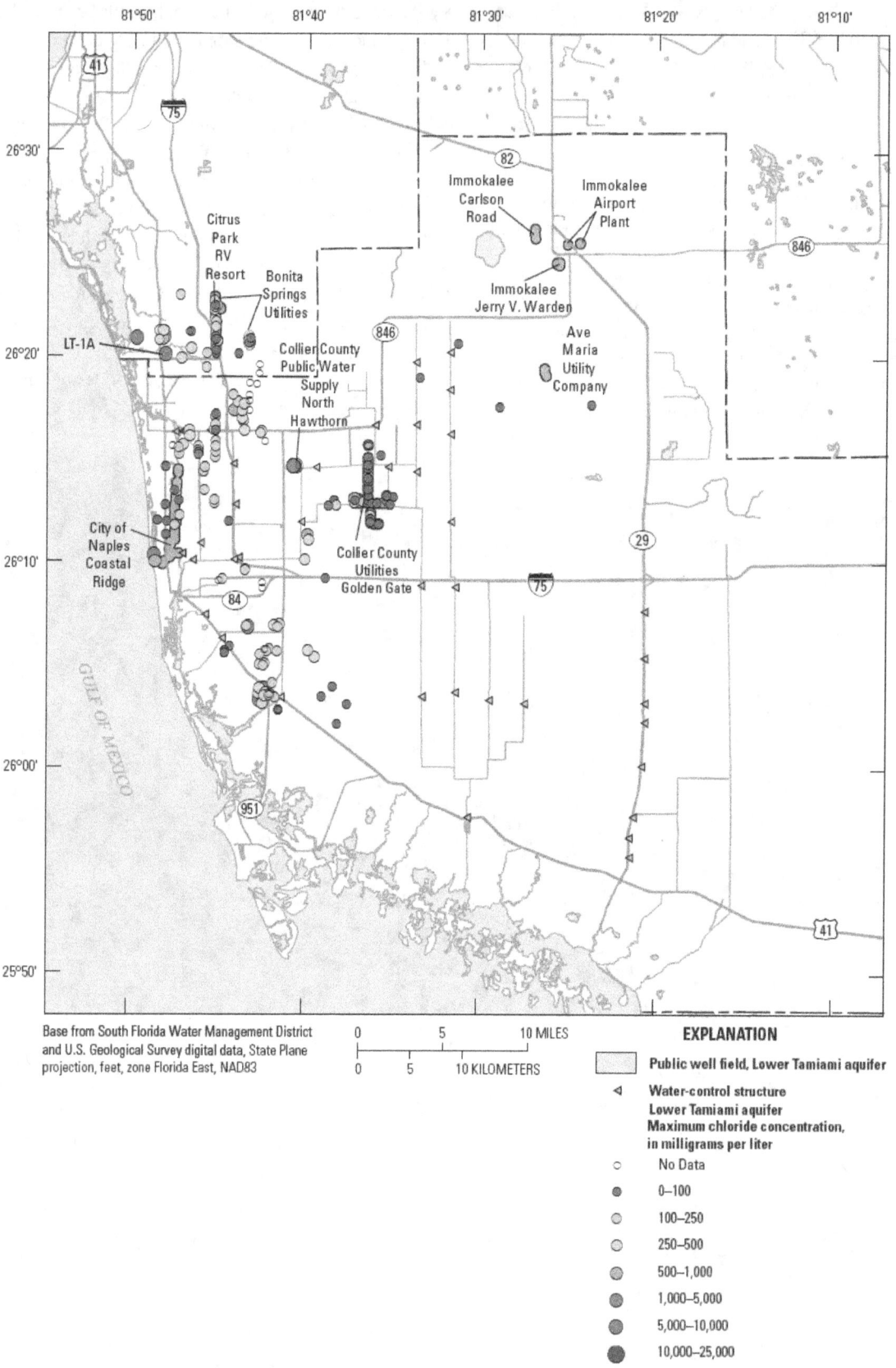

**Figure 13.**   Location of public water-supply wells and maximum chloride concentration sampled from monitoring wells open to the lower Tamiami aquifer.

East-west cross-sections *A–A'*, *B–B'*, and *C–C'* are drawn through the city of Naples Coastal Ridge and Bonita Springs well fields (figs. 14, 15, 16). The hydrostratigraphy portrayed along the axis of each cross section was interpolated from the GIS layers developed by BEM Systems Inc. (2003) and made available by the SFWMD (John Lukasiewicz, South Florida Water Management District, written commun., May 10, 2004). The GIS layers used were surfaces depicting the altitude of the land surface, and the tops of the (1) Bonita Springs marl member (aquitard layer 1), (2) Ochopee Limestone Member (aquifer layer 2), (3) upper Peace River clays (aquitard layer 2), and (4) sandstone aquifer (aquifer layer 3) (fig. 5*B*; table 1). To show as many nearby monitoring wells as possible on these cross sections, wells 0.65, 0.5, and 1.0 mi north or south of the axis of each cross section, respectively, have been superimposed on the hydrostratigraphic cross sections. These distances vary because the spatial density of the network varies. The intent was to show the information from as many wells as possible yet minimize the distance of wells from the axis of the cross section. The wells depicted on the cross sections are distributed on either side of the central axis of the cross section; therefore, the hydrostratigraphy at each monitoring well may be somewhat different than is depicted in the cross sections.

The maximum chloride concentration sampled from each well is depicted on the cross sections (figs. 14*B*, 15*B* and 16*B*) rather than the mean or minimum because protection of public water-supply wells is crucial and the maximum provides the most cautious estimate. The maximum value also provides the first indication of saltwater intrusion into an area that may not immediately be identified if the minimum or mean of data is used. Many wells indicate upward trends in chloride concentration (fig. 3); therefore, the maximum value generally represents more recent data. The approximate position of the 250 mg/L isochlor is depicted in these cross sections and is dashed where insufficient information is present. The isochlors depicted in these cross sections differ from the 250 mg/L isochlors published by the SFWMD in 2011, as described later in this report.

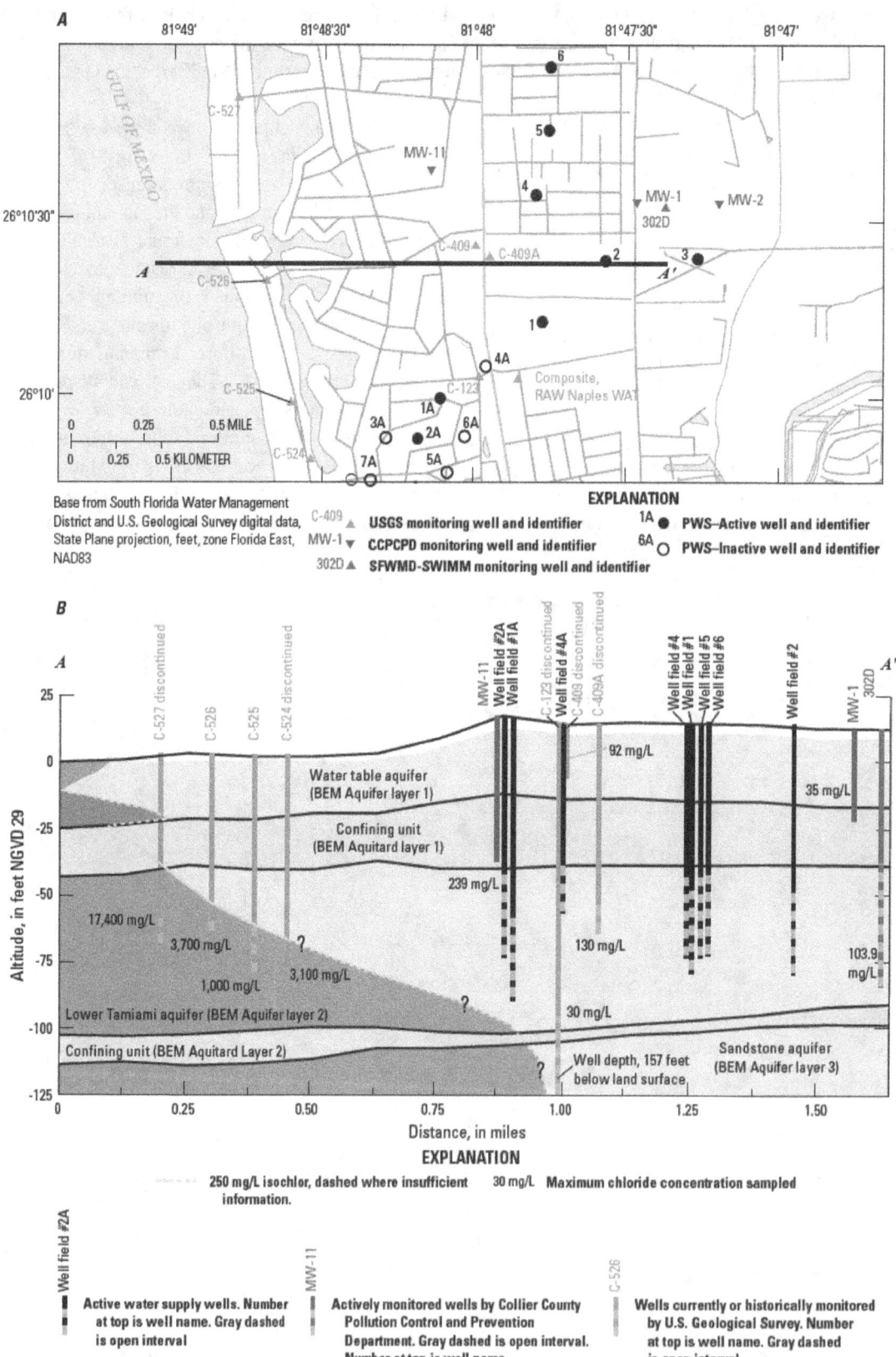

**Figure 14.**    (A) East-west cross section A to A' through the southern portion of the city of Naples Coastal Ridge well field, Collier County. (B) Cross section A to A'. Map includes monitoring wells active in 2007 and inactive USGS monitoring wells located within 0.65 mi of the axis of the cross section.

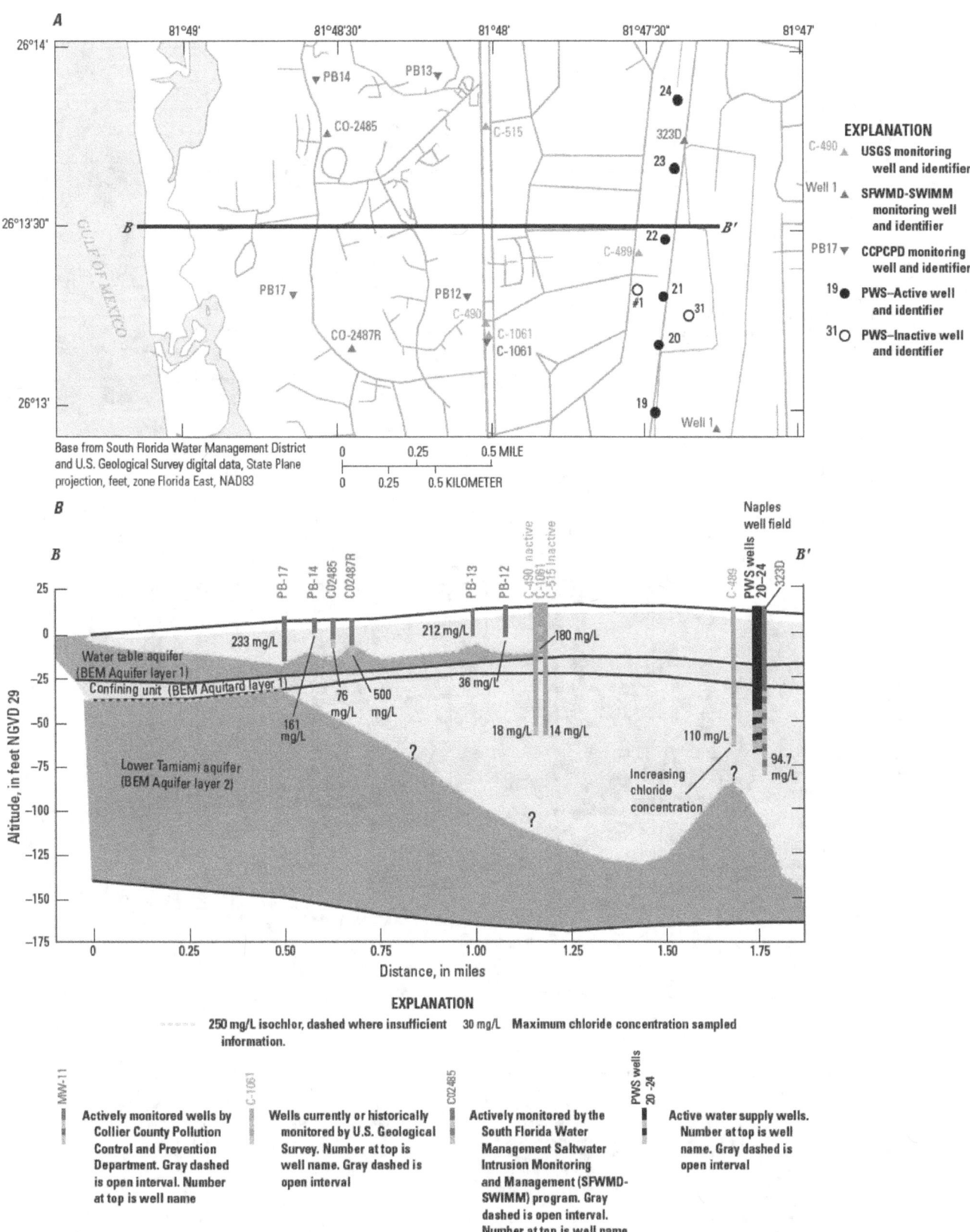

**Figure 15.** (A) East-west cross section B to B' through the north part of the city of Naples Coastal Ridge well field, Collier County. (B) Cross section B to B'. Map includes monitoring wells active in 2007 and inactive USGS monitoring wells located within 0.5 mi of the axis of the cross section.

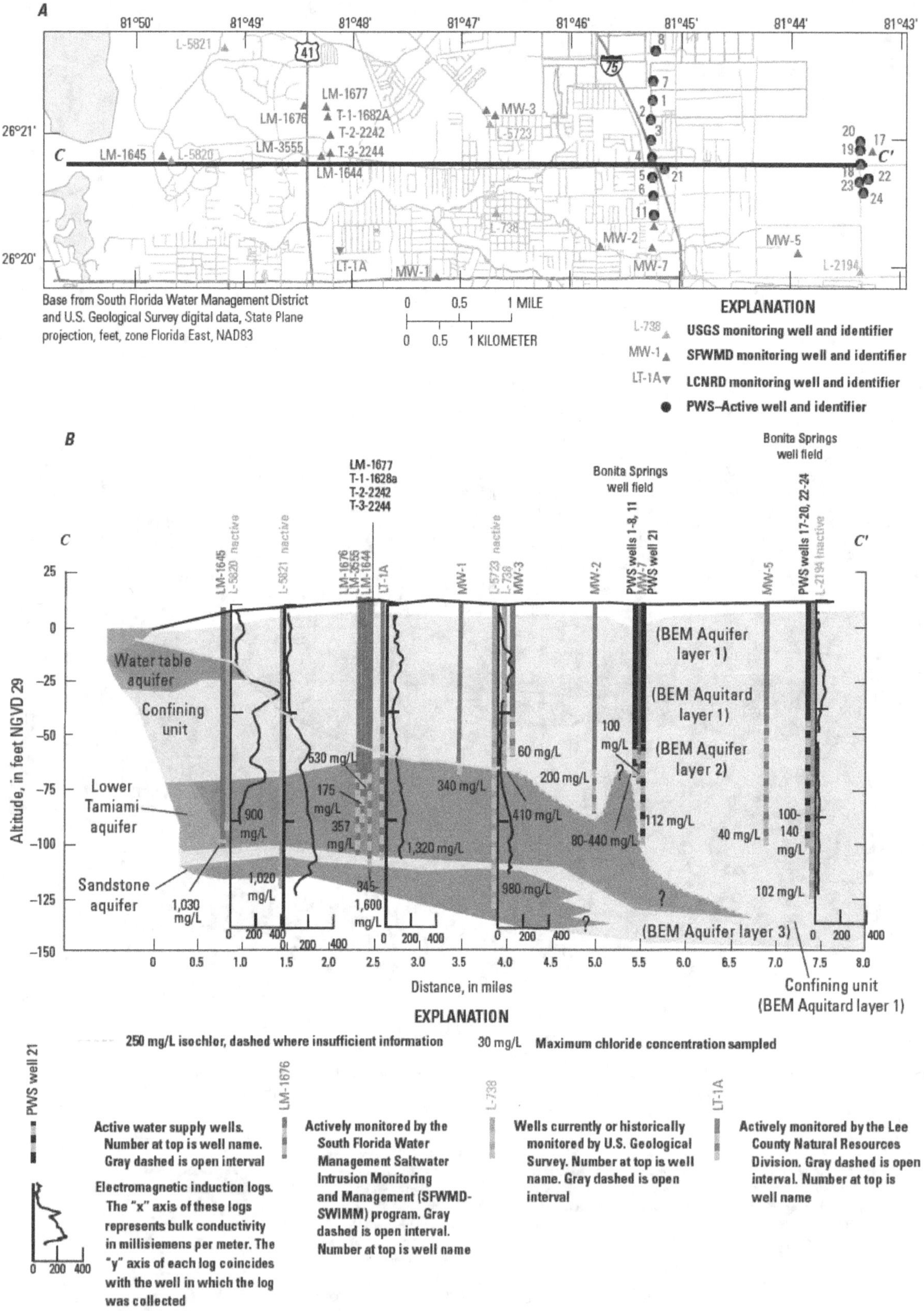

**Figure 16.**  (*A*) East-west cross section *C* to *C'* through the southern portion of the city of Bonita Springs well field, Lee County. (*B*) Cross section *C* to *C'*. Map includes monitoring wells active in 2007 and inactive USGS monitoring wells located within one mi of the axis of the cross section. Electromagnetic induction logs are depicted in the cross section.

## City of Naples Coastal Ridge Well Field

The city of Naples Coastal Ridge well field is near the coast. Increasing chloride concentration of water from wells C-489, C-516, C-525, and C-526 (fig. 3) likely indicates that the saltwater from the Gulf of Mexico is encroaching farther inland in this area, but information is insufficient to accurately show the inland extent of the 250 mg/L isochlor at the base of the lower Tamiami aquifer. Most JSWIM network monitoring wells are about the same depth or shallower than the public water-supply wells and as is evident in cross-section B–B' are completed well above the base of the lower Tamiami aquifer (fig. 15).

The chloride concentration of samples from well C-489 (figs. 3, 15) is gradually increasing. This well is located near the north part of the city of Naples Coastal Ridge well field. If these sample results are indicative of upconing beneath the well field, there is an increased likelihood of saltwater contamination of the well field. A better understanding of the source of saltwater found in well C-489 is needed.

Of the monitoring wells shown in cross-sections A–A' and B–B' (figs. 14, 15), only well C-123 (fig. 14), installed in 1952 (Klein, 1954; U.S. Geological Survey, 2012b), fully penetrates the lower Tamiami aquifer. During the 47-year period 1952 to 1999 the chloride concentration of samples from this well never exceeded 30 mg/L. The hydrogeologic framework of BEM Systems Inc. (2003) indicates, however, that 46 ft of the 60-ft open interval of well C-123 is within the thin upper semiconfining unit of the Peace River Formation and the sandstone aquifer, rather than the lower Tamiami aquifer. How this geometry affects the salinity of samples collected from this well is unknown because (1) much of the water sampled may not come from the lower Tamiami aquifer, and (2) the long open interval of this well may allow mixing of water from multiple depths. Uncertainty about the data from well C-123 and the possible existence of saltwater beneath the aquifer could probably be resolved using borehole geophysical logging.

Based in part on information from monitoring well C-123, Klein (1954, p. 35–36) interpreted that the water in the lower Tamiami aquifer beneath and immediately east of the coastal ridge was fresh. Sherwood and Klein (1961, p. 2) and Schmerge (2001, fig. 12) also interpreted an area of freshwater in the lower Tamiami aquifer beneath and immediately east of the coastal ridge. The maximum of chloride concentration of samples from well 302D (fig. 14) is 103.9 mg/L. This well nearly penetrates the aquifer, but it also has a 45 ft open interval, and is sampled using a peristaltic pump with the intake at a depth of 2 ft below the water surface. Conductivity profiles or samples collected using a nonisokinetic sampler could aid in evaluation of information from this well.

Median water-level altitudes computed using 25 years of data from USGS monitoring wells C-391, C-489, C-490, and C-516 (fig. 1) located along the coastal ridge and open to the lower Tamiami aquifer were 3.02, 2.70, 4.53, and 4.33 ft, respectively, as of April 2012 (U.S. Geological Survey,

2012b, c, d). The altitude of the base of the lower Tamiami aquifer (BEM Systems Inc., 2003) at these locations is –113, –162, –169, –126 ft, respectively. The Ghyben-Herzberg principle indicates that the freshwater head at three of these locations is sufficient or nearly sufficient to prevent saltwater from encroaching in the lower Tamiami aquifer beneath the coastal ridge. This principle, however, assumes static rather than dynamic conditions. Kohout (1964) determined that seaward flow of freshwater in coastal aquifers tends to reduce the extent of saltwater encroachment in the aquifer relative to that predicted by the Ghyben-Herzberg principle.

The modeling studies of Shoemaker and Edwards (2003) and Schlumberger (2010) indicated that, given the groundwater conditions that existed at the time of each study, the potential for lateral saltwater encroachment from the Gulf of Mexico in the lower Tamiami aquifer only extended about a mile or less from the coast in the Naples and Bonita Springs areas. Schlumberger (2010) also concluded that there was insufficient salinity information available from the lower Tamiami aquifer to properly calibrate the model, which created uncertainty in the model and its results. The potential persistence of an area of freshwater beneath the coastal ridge cannot be evaluated on an ongoing basis without active monitoring at the base of the lower Tamiami aquifer.

Many monitoring wells located between the coast and the city of Naples Coastal Ridge well field that were used by Klein (1980) to evaluate saltwater intrusion have been discontinued. Of the wells that Klein (1980) used, only wells C-489, C-490, C-491, C-516, and C-1003 (fig. 1) are currently monitored by the USGS or other agencies in the area. Even though Klein (1980) used additional wells he noted that enhanced monitoring was needed. In the lower Tamiami aquifer only a small number of additional wells are being monitored that had not been monitored by Klein (1980). These wells (fig. 1) include: (1) wells 1 and 2 monitored by the Country Club of Naples (designated CCN1 and CCN2); (2) a group of eight wells at the same location as city of Naples water-supply well 11 (designated NWS11); (3) well 1 monitored by Pine Ridge Middle School (designated PRMS1); and (4) wells 302D (fig. 14) and 323D (fig. 15). These wells do little to address the recommendations of Klein (1980) because most of the wells are either too shallow or located on the wrong side of the city of Naples Coastal well field to detect saltwater encroaching from the coast.

## Bonita Spring Utilities Well Field

Although most USGS wells depicted in cross-section C–C' through the southern part of the Bonita Springs Utilities well field (fig. 16) are no longer routinely monitored, induction logs were collected from wells L-2194 L-5723, L-5820, L-5821, and the Lee County Natural Resources Division monitoring well LT-1A in September 2008 as part of the NE1. These logs are shown in the cross section in figure 16. Water samples were also collected from these wells to evaluate chloride concentration. These logs and samples indicate that as far inland as well L-5723 the saltwater within the aquifer is about

35 ft thick. Well L-5723 is about 1.5 mi west of the well field. There are no other wells between the location of L-5723 and the well field that fully penetrate the aquifer. The maximum inland extent of saltwater in this area is unknown. The maximum chloride concentrations of samples collected from public water-supply wells 1–16 and 21 ranged from 80 to 440 mg/L, and at six of these wells concentrations were greater than 250 mg/L. It is possible, therefore, that saltwater exists beneath these supply wells and that it is upconing (fig. 16).

There are several issues that complicate the evaluation of saltwater encroachment in the aquifer near this well field:

- Only a few of the active monitoring wells east of the well field fully penetrate the aquifer.

- Based on the hydrostratigraphic interpretation of BEM Systems Inc. (2003), some of the wells, such as well L-5723, are open to both the sandstone and lower Tamiami aquifers and may allow saltwater from the sandstone aquifer to leak upward into the lower Tamiami aquifer.

- The long open intervals of the monitoring wells may allow dilution of the samples with shallow freshwater.

These issues could be addressed by (1) examination of the wells that may be open to multiple aquifers by using borehole geophysical logging, (2) abandonment of any wells that might allow leakage between aquifers, and (3) replacement of these wells with carefully designed and constructed monitoring wells that are screened at the base of the lower Tamiami aquifer.

## Mapping the Saltwater Front

The position of the saltwater front changes through time so caution should be used in interpreting rapid large-scale changes in the position of the saltwater front based on data from the existing network. The network is relatively sparse and is poorly distributed in many areas (figs. 14, 15, 16). The loss of a single well in some areas, therefore, could lead to erroneous interpretations of saltwater front movement. Variability in the salinity of water samples associated with poorly designed or maintained JSWIM network wells could erroneously be perceived as saltwater front movement. The open intervals of some of the existing monitoring wells are within the saltwater interface; accordingly, vertical changes in the saltwater interface resulting from minor changes in water levels, could result in large changes in the salinity of samples. These changes may not correspond to large-scale lateral movements in the saltwater interface.

## SFWMD Map of the 250 mg/L Isochlor

A map of the 250 mg/L ischlor in the lower Tamiami aquifer was created using salinity data collected in April and May 2009 (appendix 1). This map includes the following

caveat: "The dashed/solid red line marks an approximation of the farthest landward extent of the saltwater interface as defined by the 250 mg/L isochlor, regardless of well depth, and/or the farthest landward extent of saline surface water" (South Florida Water Management, 2011b). As previously described, well depth is an important consideration because many of the existing monitoring wells are shallower than the saltwater interface. The wells used to create the SFWMD map near the city of Naples Coastal Ridge and Bonita Springs well fields, were the same wells evaluated during the NE1 except for (1) the inactive USGS-COOP-SWIM network wells, (2) wells sampled and logged as part of the NE1, (3) wells sampled by the CCPCPD, and (4) wells 302D and 323D (table 2-3). Information from these wells provided additional information that resulted in differences in interpretation of the 250 mg/L isochlor. The same deficiencies in the JSWIM network that caused uncertainty in cross sections *A–A′*, *B–B′*, and *C–C′* (figs. 14–16) would have reduced the precision of the mapped isochlor (South Florida Water Management District, 2011b).

Aside from these considerations, there are differences between the SFWMD (2011a, b) maps and the maps developed by previous investigators.

- The SFWMD map depicts only the 250 mg/L contour. Previous investigators mapped additional isochlors (Fitzpatrick, 1986; Schmerge, 2001) that helped users differentiate between the low concentrations of chloride found in a broad area east of the coastal ridge and the high chloride concentrations typically associated with lateral encroachment of saltwater along the coast. Previous investigators, however, had more salinity data to evaluate these contours because the data included the USGS wells that are now inactive.

- The SFWMD map does not differentiate between the sources of saltwater that have been described by Klein (1954), McCoy (1962), Sherwood and Klein (1961), Klein (1980), and Schmerge (2001). Schmerge (2001) differentiated between the coastal intrusion of saltwater from the Gulf of Mexico and the saline water of connate origin or from deep upward artesian leakage (Sherwood and Klein, 1961) in the Big Cypress Basin east of the coastal ridge. The 250 mg/L isochlor depicted by the SFWMD (2011b), therefore, is drawn through saltwater bodies that may be emanating from different sources.

- The SFWMD map (2011b) indicates that the 250 mg/L isochlor extends as far inland as 10 mi, which generally agrees with the assessments of McCoy (1962, 1972), but it does not show the area of freshwater beneath the coastal ridge depicted by Klein (1954, p. 35–36), Sherwood and Klein (1961, p. 2), and Schmerge (2001, fig. 12). This difference in contours may be because the SFWMD map did not include data from deeper wells, such as well C-123, which are no longer actively monitored. Results of samples collected

January 28 and February 25, 2011, from well 302D suggest that the aquifer beneath the well field may be fresh. The quality of this data is uncertain, however, because of the method of sampling and the length of the open interval. The issues that have led to uncertainties in the location of the 250 mg/L isochlor could be resolved if the JSWIM network is enhanced as described in this report.

## Redundancy

Greater efficiency could be obtained by eliminating the redundant well sampling by multiple agencies. Some organizations collect water-quality samples to evaluate other constituents, and the sampling methods used may be mandatory for those constituents, but are not optimal for saltwater intrusion monitoring. A second sample could be collected to evaluate groundwater salinity and eliminate the sampling redundancy.

## New Monitoring Wells

The main goal of a SWIMM network is to monitor saltwater intrusion and provide the information necessary for making management decisions. Network wells will need to be strategically located, designed, and sampled to provide the quality of data necessary to answer the following questions:

- Is saltwater currently contaminating any public water-supply wells or other permitted water supplies?

- How close is the saltwater interface to the well fields?

- Is the saltwater interface advancing or retreating and at what rate?

- Is the saltwater identified at a given location currently entering the aquifer or is it a remnant of previous intrusion?

- Is saltwater moving through preferential flow paths or along the base of a given aquifer?

- What is the source of the saltwater detected at a given location?

A variety of monitoring is needed to answer the above questions:

- Public and private water-supply wells need to be sampled on a routine basis to detect saltwater intrusion.

- A series of test boreholes are needed to locate the saltwater front and determine its distance from the well field or well fields of interest.

- Additional closely spaced monitoring wells are needed to tightly bracket the saltwater front to detect its advances or retreats.

- A line of wells perpendicular to the front are needed to evaluate the overall rate of travel of the salinity front between wells.

- Well nests are needed to evaluate any movement of saltwater through preferential flow paths.

- Wells are needed to evaluate the sources of saltwater.

The existing JSWIM network largely addresses the first of these monitoring needs. This monitoring would likely detect saltwater contamination of public water-supply wells, irrigation wells, and private water-supply wells, if it occurs. Wells that have been designed specifically to answer the remaining questions, however, are few in number, poorly distributed, and are commonly old and in poor condition.

Continual evaluation of any network is required because the temporal distribution of salinity in the aquifers can change (fig. 3). Currently, an estimated 47 wells are needed to provide the appropriate spatial coverage to address some of the deficiencies in the existing network. It is impossible to determine the quantity and locations of the monitoring wells needed to map the saltwater front and to differentiate between the sources of saltwater intrusion because of the paucity of information concerning distribution of saltwater in the aquifers. Numerous test wells or surface geophysical soundings may be needed to determine exactly where each of the final monitoring wells would be installed. Modifications to the proposed plan, including changes to the number of monitoring wells required, may be required based on the findings of test well drilling or geophysical examinations. The test wells or borings could be abandoned immediately or in some instances completed as monitoring wells for future use.

The plan assumes that each of the 47 wells will be cased with PVC, have 5-ft-long screened intervals installed at the base of the aquifers, and monitored using borehole induction tools so changes in salinity above the base of the aquifer will be detected. If nested wells are used to provide information at multiple depths, additional monitoring wells will be needed. The estimate of 47 wells also assumes that sufficient hydrostratigraphic evaluation and borehole geophysical data collection will be conducted to ensure wells are screened at the base of the aquifer and not above or below it. An incremental approach was designed to indicate where additional monitoring wells may be needed. As shown in figure 17, network coverage could be improved by enhancing the monitoring program in four spatially distributed phases (fig. 17).

The objective of Phase 1 is to identify potential saltwater intrusion at the city of Naples Coastal Ridge well field. This area is proposed for improvement in the first phase because the saltwater front is known to be relatively close to this well field although the exact location is uncertain. Increases in the salinity of samples from some monitoring wells located near or within the well field indicate an urgent need to understand the exact location of the saltwater front, and the source of saltwater in these wells. The construction of 10 new monitoring wells should provide the necessary long-term monitoring

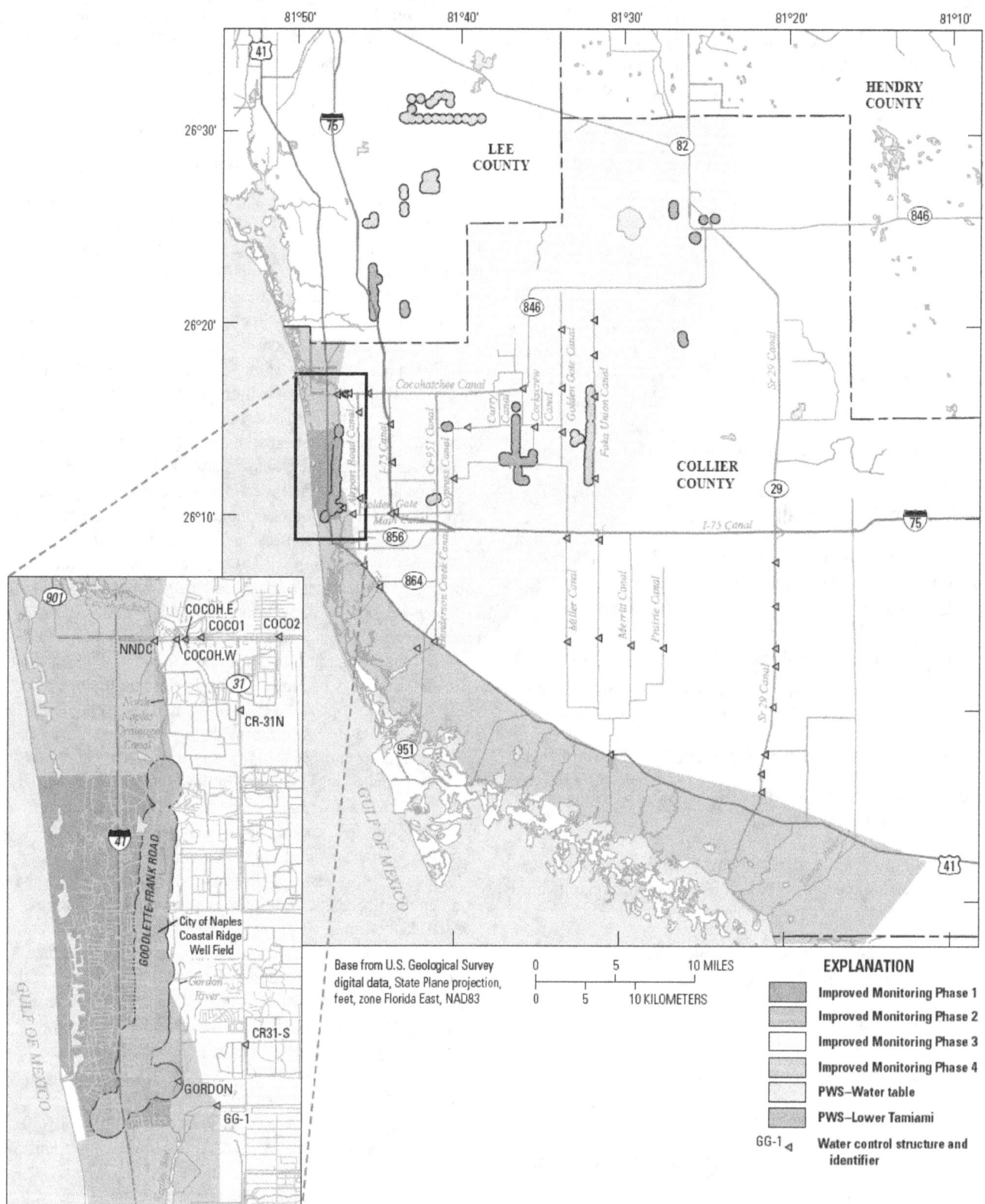

**Figure 17.** Areas where additional monitoring is needed to evaluate the potential threat of saltwater intrusion to well fields, evaluate the sources of saltwater in the aquifer, and map the extent of saltwater in the surficial aquifer system.

in this area. These monitoring wells could bracket the saltwater interface in up to five locations including: four paired wells placed along the length of the city of Naples Coastal Ridge well field to evaluate lateral encroachment of saltwater from the Gulf of Mexico, and one pair of wells to evaluate the leakage of saltwater from the Gordon River downstream of the salinity control structure. Ideally, paired wells need to be installed in areas where well field withdrawals are the greatest and where active public water supply wells are close to the coast. Test drilling or surface geophysical measurements can provide critical information about the complexity of the saltwater interface in this area. This information can be used to increase or decrease the number of well pairs used.

Phase 2 will assess whether saline canal flow inland of the salinity control structures near the city of Naples Coastal Ridge well field may elevate groundwater salinity. Two new wells are proposed to be sited along the Gordon River upstream from the salinity control structure and between the city of Naples Coastal Ridge well field and the river, and one well drilled between the North Naples Drainage Canal and the city of Naples Coastal Ridge well field.

Phase 3 is designed to evaluate saltwater leakage between aquifers and the movement of connate saltwater near the well fields that are located farther inland in Collier County. Eight new wells are estimated to be needed for this evaluation, but the number of wells would ultimately depend on how many areas of leakage are identified by test drilling or surface geophysical measurements and the extents of these areas.

Phase 4 will provide the wide monitoring network needed to map lateral saltwater encroachment from the Gulf of Mexico along the base of the lower Tamiami and water-table aquifers throughout Collier County. Twenty-six monitoring wells are proposed to be installed with the majority completed in the lower Tamiami aquifer because currently numerous wells are available that fully penetrate the water-table aquifer. Although additional wells may be needed to monitor salinity within the lower Tamiami aquifer, the new wells and geophysical measurements will provide a good framework to understanding the complexity of the extent of lateral encroachment from the Gulf of Mexico into the lower Tamiami aquifer. The number of wells monitored on a routine basis for mapping can then be increased or decreased as needed. Part of this area is remote, and saltwater intrusion may be more efficiently evaluated using airborne geophysical surveys.

The network could be improved by (1) additional monitoring activities at existing monitoring wells, (2) application of surface and airborne geophysical techniques, and (3) collection of salinity data from surface-water bodies.

## Airborne, Surface, and Borehole Geophysics, Coring, and Aquifer Testing

Existing hydrostratigraphic information in southwest Florida is mostly based on sample cuttings collected during drilling activities, supplemented with some aquifer-test and borehole geophysical data. Advances in borehole, surface, and airborne geophysical methods have provided new information that has greatly improved carbonate aquifer characterizations in south Florida. Geophysical methods that could be applied in southwest Florida to evaluate the hydrostratigraphic framework of the aquifers include high-resolution seismic-reflection surveying (Cunningham and others, 2001b, 2003), borehole geophysical logging, and electrical or electromagnetic geophysical methods, such as (1) direct current (DC) resistivity measurements, (2) continuous resistivity profiling (CRP), (3) electromagnetic induction logging, (4) time-domain electromagnetic (TEM) measurements, (5) capacitively coupled resistivity survey profiling, and (6) helicopter electromagnetic (HEM) surveys. These geophysical methods can be combined with analyses of core and aquifer tests to greatly improve the quality of hydrostratigraphic information available.

## High-Resolution Seismic-Reflection Surveys

One of the difficulties in developing an accurate hydrostratigraphic interpretation of south Florida is that geologic strata in many instances do not overlie each other as a series of horizontal, continuous layers with uniform lithologic character. High-resolution seismic reflection studies conducted in south Florida have revealed complex subsurface features, including erosional truncation, toplap, onlap, or downlap relations established during erosion and deposition of the geologic strata, as well as seismic-sag structural systems resulting from a progressive evolution from cave formation, to cave collapse, and ultimately suprastratal collapse (Cunningham and Walker, 2009). Commonly the strata slope in a uniform direction, similar to a stack of tilted playing cards. It is difficult, therefore, to correlate strata between test wells that are a substantial distance from each another.

A combination of high-resolution, seismic-reflection surveying and analyses of core from test wells including nanofossil biostratigraphy and strontium-isotope chemostratigraphy have been used in southwest Florida to improve understanding of the regional hydrostratigraphic relations (Cunningham and others, 2001a, 2001b, 2003). Expanded use of these methods could resolve some of the existing uncertainty of hydrostratigraphic interpretation within the study area. Seismic surveys like these have been conducted in several of the large canals in south Florida as well as offshore.

## Time-Series Electromagnetic Induction Log Datasets

Electronic or electromagnetic methods are useful in detecting and mapping saltwater in aquifers because saltwater conducts electricity better than freshwater. Electromagnetic induction logging equipment (ASTM International, 2001) provides a maximum response from aquifer materials in a donut-shaped radius that extends 8 to 40 inches from the center of the monitoring well (McNeill, 1990). Electromagnetic induction borehole data can be collected in wells that are fully cased with PVC, accordingly, electromagnetic logging equipment can provide measurements of bulk conductivity and bulk resistivity of aquifer materials every tenth of a foot for the full depth interval of a monitoring well, without the uncertainties caused by flow or mixing within long open intervals. Bulk resistivity is the inverse of bulk conductivity. The bulk conductivity measured is dependent on the electrical properties of the rock and the water in the rock and varies with porosity. The porosity and electrical conductivity of the rock or sediments themselves generally do not change substantially through time. The changes observed in temporally successive induction logs are related to temporal changes in the pore water conductivity. In this way, induction logs can be used in a similar fashion to a series of water conductivity profiles. A series of electromagnetic induction logs can be converted to time-series electromagnetic induction log (TSEMIL) datasets by eliminating the offsets caused by small differences in calibration (figs. 18 and 19). Chloride concentration sampled and bulk conductivity measured by electromagnetic induction from well G-3609 increased near the base of the aquifer as saltwater encroached landward (fig. 18). During the 16 year period 1996–2011, G-3601 bulk conductivity steadily increased between the depths of 140 and 190 ft bls as saltwater gradually encroached within the aquifer (fig. 19A). The TSEMIL dataset from well G-3601 also show influxes of conductive water in the depth intervals of 60 to 100 ft bls (2003 and 2004) and 100 to 130 ft bls (2009).

Wells can be designed specifically for TSEMIL collection (fig. 20). Prior to well completion, geophysical logs and recovered core are used to evaluate the stratigraphy, detect preferential flow zones within the aquifer, and determine where secondary filter packs may be required. This information is used to determine the exact strata into which the screen interval should be installed to provide optimal information. Small sampling tubes installed into separate filter packs (fig. 20) replace the multidepth sampling of the old open-borehole wells and eliminate the potential of ambient well-bore flow. Monitoring wells can be designed to fully penetrate an aquifer so that the changes in salinity throughout the thickness of the aquifer can be evaluated and the maximum landward extent of saltwater can be determined.

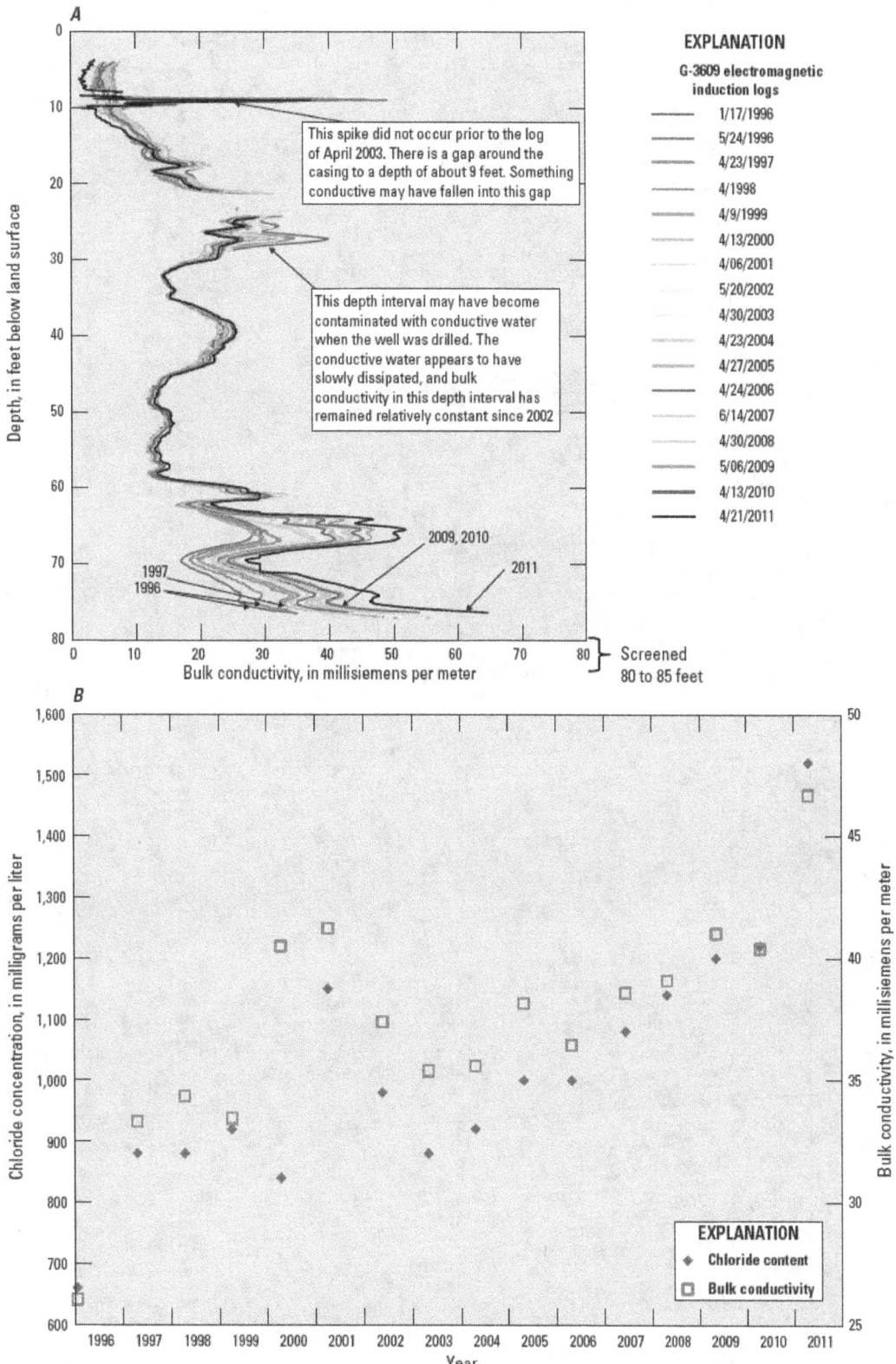

**Figure 18.** (*A*) a time-series electromagnetic induction log dataset collected from monitoring well G-3609 in Miami-Dade County and (*B*) results of chloride concentration samples from well G-3609, and the bulk conductivity at a depth of 74.5 feet.

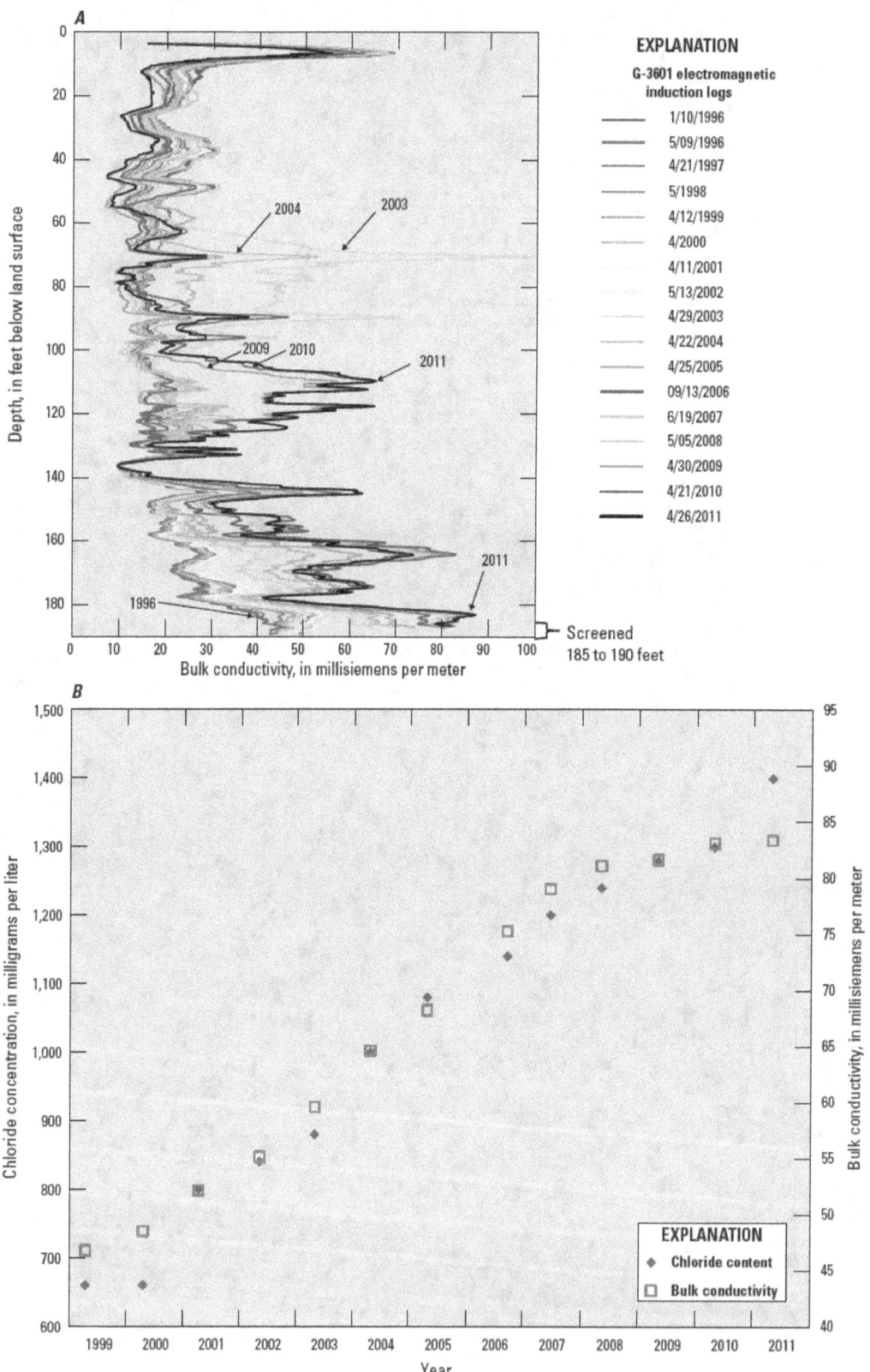

**Figure 19.**    (A) a time-series electromagnetic induction log dataset collected at G-3601 in Miami-Dade County and (B) results of chloride concentration samples from well G-3601 and bulk conductivity measured at a depth of 184 feet.

Depths of screen intervals, and seals are based on results of geophysical logging

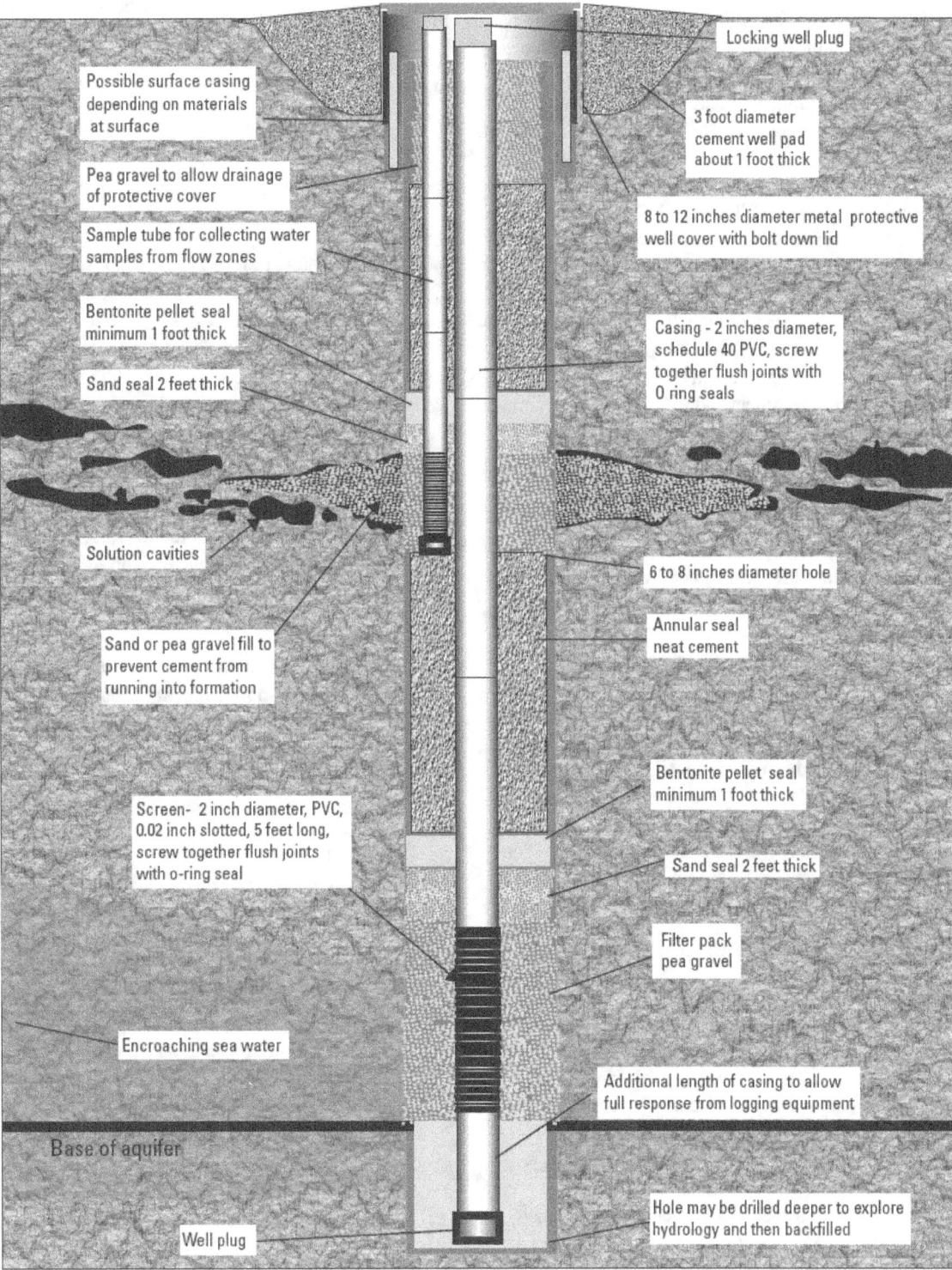

**Figure 20.**   Schematic of a well designed for time-series electromagnetic induction logging.

## Time-Domain Electromagnetic Soundings

Time-domain electromagnetic (TEM) soundings have been used extensively since 1994 to evaluate the landward extent of saltwater in aquifers in south Florida (Sonenshein, 1997, Fitterman and others, 1999; Hittle, 1999; Schmerge, 2001; Stewart and others, 2002; Fitterman and Prinos, 2011) and to aid in the calibration and interpretation of results from helicopter-based electromagnetic (HEM) surveys conducted in the Everglades (Fitterman and Deszcz-Pan, 1998, 2002) and the Model Land Area (Fitterman and others, 2012).

The primary reason for collecting TEM soundings in the Biscayne aquifer in Miami-Dade County was to evaluate the inland extent of saltwater in shallow aquifers. However, Fitterman and Prinos (2011) discovered that many of the models of these soundings have a layer interface that corresponds closely with the base of the Biscayne aquifer. TEM soundings might also be used in the Big Cypress Basin both to evaluate the extent of saltwater encroachment and to refine the hydrostratigraphic framework.

## Helicopter Electromagnetic Surveys

Helicopter electromagnetic (HEM) surveys can provide information similar to that obtained by TEM soundings. This information can be used to interpret the occurrence and extent of saltwater in earth materials. HEM surveys were completed in 1994 and 2001 in south and southeast Florida (Fitterman and Deszcz-Pan, 1998, 2002; Fitterman and others, 2012). These surveys provide a 3-dimensional model of the distribution of saltwater in these areas. Another HEM survey conducted in 2001 includes part of the Big Cypress Basin (Fitterman and Deszcz-Pan, 2002), but the data were never fully processed. These data could prove valuable for evaluating saltwater intrusion in a portion of the Big Cypress Basin too remote for conventional monitoring.

## Borehole Geophysical Logging

Recent studies conducted by the USGS show that some limestone aquifers can be more accurately conceptualized as dual-porosity aquifers (Renken and others, 2008; Cunningham and others, 2009). As the name implies, dual-porosity aquifers comprise materials having two different types of porosity: (1) matrix porosity (inter-particle pores and separate vugs), that may provide groundwater storage, and (2) touching-vug macroporosity, or bedding-plane and cavernous vugs, vertical solution pipes, and solution-enlarged fractures, which may create concentrated groundwater flow zones at various depths within an aquifer (Cunningham and Sukop, 2011). The effect of highly permeable flow zones on the geometry of the saltwater interface is poorly understood. If a flow zone were to intersect both the intakes of public water-supply wells in a well field and the saltwater interface it could potentially provide pathways for saltwater to contaminate the well field

more readily than if the saltwater interface were in a homogeneous isotropic aquifer. Collection of additional borehole geophysical data in existing wells and collection of borehole geophysical data (Wacker and Cunningham, 2008), coring, and sampling during well installation can improve understanding of the distribution of these flow zones. Borehole data that may provide valuable information include the following:

- **Vertical flow data** can be used to evaluate the quality of salinity sample results collected from long open-borehole intervals and to examine interaquifer flow that may occur in wells open to multiple aquifers. Flow data collected at each borehole under ambient (static) and dynamic (pumping) conditions would allow for the estimation of transmissivity. Several different types of flow meters are available, including (1) the electromagnetic flow meter, (2) the heat pulse flow meter, and (3) the spinner flow meter. Each meter has benefits and weaknesses. Collection of a suite of flow meter data generally provides the best results.

- **Borehole image logs.** It is not possible to collect core from wells that have already been drilled. If a well has a long open-borehole interval, however, optical or acoustic borehole image logs provide a virtual inspection of geologic section that can be used to refine the framework.

- **Electromagnetic induction/natural gamma-ray/ spontaneous potential/single-point resistance data** can help indicate where confining clays are present. Electromagnetic induction data can be collected in PVC cased wells. This information can be used to evaluate whether a well has penetrated a confining layer or not.

- **Full waveform sonic data** can be collected in unscreened wells with long open-borehole intervals to generate a vertical log of compressional and Stoneley wave velocities. Compressional wave velocities are used in the Wylie or Raymer-Hunt equations to compute sonic porosity. Stoneley waves are low frequency, large-amplitude surface waves that propagate along the walls of fluid-filled boreholes during sonic logging. These wave velocities can be cautiously used for qualitative estimates of permeability of the rock surrounding the borehole. Generally, low amplitudes can represent relatively high permeability, and high amplitudes can represent relatively low permeability.

- **Water-quality data** can indicate where water of differing chemical compositions enter or depart the well bore. This information can provide insights concerning how water flows through the aquifer and can be used to evaluate the effects of vertical flow on collected salinity information.

## Coring and Aquifer Tests

An improved understanding of dual-porosity groundwater flow within the macroporous limestone of the Biscayne aquifer has been developed within the context of a cyclostratigraphic framework (Renken and others, 2008; Cunningham and others, 2009; Cunningham and Sukop, 2011). This analysis has been accomplished through combined use and analysis of rock-core samples, borehole geophysical data, and hydraulic tests. Similar information obtained within the Big Cypress Basin can aid in the development of groundwater flow and solute transport models used to understand the potential of saltwater intrusion. Rock core samples provide detailed information about subsurface lithologic conditions at specific borehole locations that cannot be obtained from borehole geophysical data alone. Improvements in understanding the cyclostratigraphy require continuously cored test wells and digital optical borehole image logs. Where core recovery is incomplete, optical borehole image logs can be used to determine the exact depths of partial core sections.

Collection of data during slug tests, specific yields tests, or aquifer tests, and analysis of these data can be used to identify aquifer and confining units and to quantity the transmissivity, specific storage, and hydraulic conductivity.

## Quality-Assurance Measures

Salinity data provided by the JSWIM network are collected by multiple organizations. Uniformity in data quality and collection procedures would ultimately provide scientifically defensible information regarding the location of the interface. Management of the JSWIM network could be improved through organizational planning meetings that (1) poll network participants about sampling, processing, storage, and quality-assurance/quality-control (QA/QC) protocols, (2) examine trends in salinity, water levels, and withdrawals of water from the aquifer to evaluate changes in the extent of, or potential for, saltwater intrusion, (3) evaluate resources available for network improvements, (4) establish the responsibilities of network participants, (5) establish a schedule of improvements (see next section for an example), and (6) develop a JSWIM network QA/QC plan. Quality-assurance protocols (Florida Department of Environmental Protection, 2008b; U.S. Geological Survey, variously dated) that may help in development of the JSWIM QA/QC plan include the following:

- Provide training in the equipment used and the applicable SOPs to ensure that samples are properly collected.

- Create and use field forms for the collection of water-quality samples. The FDEP describes what must be recorded for each sample (Florida Department of Environmental Protection, 2008b).

- Compute volume of water in the well when it is necessary to purge a well because this volume depends on the water level in the well. FDEP describes how to compute the well volume (Florida Department of Environmental Protection, 2008b).

- Periodically review new incoming data. Create long-term data plots to identify trends or detect any data offsets that result from improperly collected samples or are due to well damage.

- Create and use station problem report forms to record problems at a monitoring well that affect the security of the well or the quality of samples collected from it. These problems may be evident from visual inspection of the well, analysis of the data, or annual well depth checks. These problems are evaluated by a manager and measures are taken to address the problems. If a problem cannot be corrected and affects the quality of samples, a decision may be made to discontinue a specific well.

- Prepare brief annual synopsis of the data collected from each well, documenting:: (1) the number of samples collected, (2) samples that may have been rejected upon review, (3) techniques and equipment used for sampling, (4) outstanding problems with the condition of the well, and (5) actions taken during the year to address any well condition problems.

- Periodically accompany technicians in the field to evaluate their sampling techniques.

- Annually analyze blind samples to ensure that analysts have the skill and training necessary to provide high-quality sample analyses.

- Review field and office procedures every 3 years to ensure proper sampling methodology and documentation of results.

- Ensure that all documentation concerning the monitoring wells and samples is reviewed to verify that data are being properly collected and that all the information necessary to evaluate well location, construction, location, and sample results is being recorded.

- Verify that each organization or assigned individual is meeting their responsibilities.

These general quality-assurance procedures combined with improvements described in this report would address many of the well condition problems and sample collection problems that were identified during the NE1. These measures also help ensure that corrective actions are taken before problems result in long-term impairment of data quality. For organizations collecting only a few samples, these protocols may seem excessive. However, if the JSWIM networks include data collected by hundreds of individual organizations, each collecting only a few samples, then a large percentage of data could be impaired if the necessary sampling and quality-assurance protocols are not followed.

## Improving Data Accessibility

The data management capabilities of governmental organizations have expanded greatly during the 75-year period (1937 to 2012) during which saltwater intrusion has been monitored in southwest Florida. In the past, only paper files existed. Today, large databases maintained by the FDEP, SFWMD, and USGS organize and store the large volumes of data being collected. Data can be retrieved from these databases to allow examinations like those conducted for the NE1. Data stored electronically in formats that are relatively easy to work with are also available from some county governments. A number of weaknesses in information dissemination, however, still need to be addressed:

- **Information access.** Information from the various networks has to be requested from each organization that possesses it. Some, but not all information is available online. Personnel may have to retrieve the requested information from that organization's database or files and provide it as permitted by their own schedules. Not all organizations have staff dedicated to providing data retrievals. In some instances, repeated requests were required to obtain the necessary information for the NE1.

- **Information consolidation.** Geospatial analyses require a number of steps that have to be repeated each time an analysis is conducted, including retrieval of well construction and location information, and water-sample results from each organization. Water-level data from one site may exist in several files that have to be merged for long-term analyses.

- **Format of data.** Quantitative evaluation of trends generally requires that data be imported into statistical analysis software. Several statistical analysis packages have been developed that are well suited for the evaluation of water-quality and hydrologic information, but input data may need to be restructured to satisfy input formats.

- **Discrepancies in redundant data.** In some instances, salinity data have been collected from the same well by different organizations. Redundant sampling provides a good quality-assurance check, but organizations are not necessarily aware of other agency data collection activities. These redundancies are further complicated by inconsistent well names. Differences were also identified in the data provided for the same well by different organizations. These differences could lead to incorrect interpretation.

These weaknesses in information dissemination can increase the difficulty of compiling all available information needed for timely, ongoing, managerial evaluations, particularly if immediate decisions are required. These issues have to be considered whenever an organization needs an analysis of the status of saltwater intrusion.

To provide decision makers with readily accessible information concerning the landward extent of saltwater in the aquifer, the USGS developed a prototype Web site (U.S. Geological Survey, 2012d) for Miami-Dade County. Features of this Web site include:

- An Arc-IMS operating system provides geographical information in a similar fashion to most GIS applications. Layers showing hydrology, transportation, utilities, and boundary information can be viewed or not. This system allows panning, zooming, measuring, and identification of geographic features.

- Layers are included that show the previously mapped landward extent of intrusion, locations of monitoring wells, and locations of public water-supply wells.

- Symbology is used to geographically show the chloride concentration of recent samples from monitoring wells and to show the long-term trend.

- Information from ongoing sampling is automatically updated, which keeps the Web site current.

- Arc-IMS layers provided on the Web site can be linked directly to a user's GIS system and automatically updated. This linkage allows the examination of the most current salinity information relative to the users' own GIS layers.

A similar tool would be useful for evaluating the results of the JSWIM network in southwest Florida and could permit improved oversight of saltwater intrusion monitoring activities. Before such a tool is implemented, it would be helpful to standardize the quality of the JSWIM network data and to establish a single vertical and horizontal datum. If all data are being collected to the same standards, and if these data are consolidated into a similar format, then Web-based analytical tools could greatly improve the ease of data analysis.

# Prioritization of Network Improvements

The prioritization of network improvements generally depends on several factors that include (1) available resources, (2) information that becomes available as improvements are incrementally completed, and (3) needs and priorities of the organizations operating the network. The iterative plan depicted in table 2 proposes modest improvements over 6 years. By its completion, only 8 to 15 new wells would be added, which should satisfy information needs to address phases 1 and 2 (fig. 17) of the proposed plan to improve spatial coverage. Additional iterations, however, would be needed to provide spatial coverage required for phases 3 and 4 (fig. 17).

In table 2, network management improvements are highlighted in green. Quality-assurance improvements and training are highlighted in yellow. Items highlighted in orange (table 2) are contingent on the desires of resource managers. If resource managers plan to continue to use older wells and long-screened wells for the foreseeable future, these contingency items would be necessary to verify that data of reasonable quality can be obtained from these older wells. If resource managers wish to expedite the installation of new wells, however, then these evaluations can potentially be curtailed in

areas where existing long-screened wells would be replaced by new wells of an improved design. Items highlighted in grey (table 2) are improvements in monitoring and refinement of the hydrostratigraphic framework. Each year, small improvements to the network are made through the limited collection of surface and borehole geophysical data and installation of a few new wells. Surface geophysical measurements or test wells are proposed to aid in the selection of exact locations for monitoring wells. The first geophysical measurements could serve as a pilot effort, and subsequent measurements could be conducted if the pilot effort proved successful. Improved data dissemination is highlighted in blue and considered an optional measure (table 2).

Implementation of the full JSWIM network improvement plan proposed in this report would require the combined efforts of each organization. Cooperation between these organizations can potentially provide benefits that no single organization can accomplish on its own. For example, the USGS relied on a cooperative relation with numerous Federal, State, county, and city partners in southwest Florida to establish the first SWIM network and to publish numerous studies that were used to help develop and manage the existing water supply. Although the USGS is a minor partner in the JSWIM network, the remaining organizations can still work together to improve the JSWIM network. The resulting information could help cities and counties protect their water resources.

**Table 2.**  Proposed 6-year plan to improve the quality of saltwater intrusion monitoring activities in southwest Florida.

| Component | Desired improvement | FY2013 | FY2014 | FY2015 | FY2016 | FY2017 | FY2018 |
|---|---|---|---|---|---|---|---|
| 1 | Conduct a survey of sampling, processing, storage, and quality assurace. | | | | | | |
| 2 | Conduct an organiztional planning meeting | | | | | | |
| 3 | Develop Standard Operating Proceedures specifically for salinity sampling. | | | | | | |
| 4 | Develop a joint saltwater intrusion monitoring (JSWIM) network quality assurace plan. | | | | | | |
| 5 | Evaluate and determine a schedule of desired network improvements. | | | | | | |
| 6 | Develop a schedule to address well condition or missing information issues. | | | | | | |
| 7 | Establish a training program. | | | | | | |
| 8 | Evaluate known JSWIM well condition issues | | | | | | |
| 9 | Conduct a well inventory to identify any wells that could be added to fill gaps in the JSWIM network. | | | | | | |
| 10 | Implement annual well depth checks | | | | | | |
| 11 | Begin training and quality assurance measures | | | | | | |
| 12 | Update aquifer assignments | | | | | | |
| 13 | Begin monitoring canal salinity | | | | | | |
| 14 | Detailed borehole geophysical logging of 1 long screened well | | | | | | |
| 15 | Collect 4 to 6 electrical or electromagnetic surface geophysical measurments* or drill test wells | | | | | | |
| 16 | Collect and process high-resolution seismic reflection data* | | | | | | |
| 17 | Install 2-3 new wells | | | | | | |
| 18 | Collect and analyze core from new wells | | | | | | |
| 19 | Collect and process detailed borehole geophysical and water quality logs from new wells | | | | | | |
| 20 | Collect Oxygen, hydrogen, and strontium stable isotope samples | | | | | | |
| 21 | Create scripts and website to improve data dissemination | | | | | | |
| 22 | Review of information gained in 2012 | | | | | | |
| 23 | Examine well problems with borehole camera | | | | | | |
| 24 | Repair or abandonment of damaged wells | | | | | | |
| 25 | Collect detailed geophysical logs in 10 long screened wells | | | | | | |

**Table 2.** Proposed 6-year plan to improve the quality of saltwater intrusion monitoring activities in southwest Florida.

| Component | Desired improvement | FY2013 | FY2014 | FY2015 | FY2016 | FY2017 | FY2018 |
|---|---|---|---|---|---|---|---|
| 26 | Collect 4 to 6 electrical or electromagnetic surface geophysical measurments** or drill test wells | | | ▓ | | | |
| 27 | Collect and process high-resolution seismic reflection data** | | | ▓ | | | |
| 28 | Install 2 to 4 new wells | | | ▓ | | | |
| 29 | Collect and analyze core from new wells | | | ▓ | | | |
| 30 | Collect and process detailed borehole geophysical and water quality logs from new wells | | | ▓ | | | |
| 31 | Review of information gained in 2013 | | | | ▓ | | |
| 32 | Examine well problems with borehole camera | | | | ▓ | | |
| 33 | Repair or abandonment of damaged wells | | | | ▓ | | |
| 34 | Collect detailed geophysical logs in 10 long screened wells | | | | ▓ | | |
| 35 | Collect 4 to 6 electrical or electromagnetic surface geophysical measurments** or drill test wells | | | | ▓ | | |
| 36 | Collect and process high-resolution seismic reflection data** | | | | ▓ | | |
| 37 | Install 2 to 4 new wells | | | | ▓ | | |
| 38 | Collect and analyze core from new wells | | | | ▓ | | |
| 39 | Collect and process detailed geophysical and water quality logs from new wells | | | | ▓ | | |
| 40 | Review of information gained in 2014 | | | | | ▓ | |
| 41 | Examine well problems with borehole camera | | | | | ▓ | |
| 42 | Repair or abandonment of damaged wells | | | | | ▓ | |
| 43 | Collect detailed geophysical logs in 10 long screened wells | | | | | ▓ | |
| 44 | Collect 4 to 6 electrical or electromagnetic surface geophysical measurments** or drill test wells | | | | | ▓ | |
| 45 | Collect and process high-resolution seismic reflection data** | | | | | ▓ | |
| 46 | Collect and analyze core from new wells | | | | | ▓ | |
| 47 | Collect and process detailed borehole geophysical and water quality logs from new wells | | | | | ▓ | |
| 48 | Evaluate progress in network improvement and revise as needed | | | | | | ▓ |

**Table 2.**  Proposed 6-year plan to improve the quality of saltwater intrusion monitoring activities in southwest Florida.

| Component | Desired improvement | FY2013 | FY2014 | FY2015 | FY2016 | FY2017 | FY2018 |
|---|---|---|---|---|---|---|---|
| 49 | Ongoing quality assurance review of JSWIM participants | | | | | | |
| 50 | Ongoing annual total depth well checks | | | | | | |
| 51 | Long term collection of oxygen, hydrogen, and strontium stable isotope samples. | | | | | | |
| 52 | Long term Time-Series Electromagnetic Induction logging | | | | | | |
| 53 | Long term canal salinity monitoring | | | | | | |

* During the first year the value of electrical, electromagnetic, and seismic surface geophysical techniques could be evaluated.

** Dependent on evaluations conducted during the first year.

# Summary

During the mid-20th century, saline groundwater intruded coastal surficial aquifers of southwest Florida that had previously contained freshwater. Analyses of water samples from monitoring wells near to the saltwater interface indicate that saline groundwater is still intruding some areas. The causes of this intrusion are (1) encroachment of saltwater along the base of aquifers caused by reductions in freshwater head from water-supply withdrawals or canal drainage, (2) infiltration from tidal marshes, estuaries, and bays, (3) the migration of saltwater upstream from unregulated canals or streams during drought periods and the leakage of this water into surficial aquifers, (4) movement of residual saltwater that entered the aquifer during previous sea-level high stands occurring during interglacial periods, and (5) upward seepage through leaky confining units and poorly sealed wells. The Joint Saltwater Intrusion Monitoring (JSWIM) network is used by water managers to monitor the extent and distribution of saltwater in the aquifers. The largest component of the JSWIM network is the South Florida Water Management District-Saltwater Intrusion Monitoring and Management (SFWMD-SWIMM) network. The phase 1 examination of existing salinity monitoring in southwest Florida (NE1) was conducted to evaluate the JSWIM network. This examination identified the following deficiencies in the JSWIM network:

- Monitoring is predominantly clustered around the well fields.

- Monitoring is dense in some areas but sparse in some areas where it is needed such as near the saltwater front.

- Monitoring relies on a large percentage of wells that were neither designed nor intended to be used specifically for monitoring of saltwater intrusion in the aquifers or evaluation of the sources of saltwater.

- Many monitoring wells are generally too shallow to provide water samples from the depths necessary to evaluate the extent and distribution of saltwater intrusion in the lower Tamiami aquifer.

- Many monitoring wells have long-screened or open-hole intervals in which water may flow vertically under ambient conditions and cause dilution of samples.

- Many monitoring wells are missing construction information, such as well depth or cased depth.

- Florida Department of Environmental Protection Standard Operating Procedures (SOPs) call for sampling of long open-interval wells by pumping from near the top of the water column or top of the open interval, which could result in samples that are not representative of maximum salinity in the aquifer.

- Obstructed or damaged wells could provide samples that are not fully representative of aquifer conditions. Some partially obstructed wells are still sampled.

- There are inconsistencies between the depths of some JSWIM network wells and the aquifers to which these wells are considered to be open. This may be related to differences between previous and current hydrostratigraphic interpretations.

- Surface-water salinity sampling in some areas is insufficient to evaluate whether saltwater occurs in some canals near coastal well fields.

- Existing monitoring generally cannot differentiate between the multiple sources of saltwater intrusion in the aquifers of the study area.

- Some of the technological advancements that can improve the quality of salinity monitoring, such as the use of nonisokinetic samplers and the collection of time-series electromagnetic induction log (TSEMIL) datasets, have not been used.

- Some monitoring is redundant.

- Data dissemination mechanisms often require time consuming compilation and post processing efforts before saltwater intrusion can be evaluated.

- Quality assurance of the network as a whole needs improvement.

A plan to improve saltwater intrusion monitoring in southwest Florida has been developed that includes the following elements:

- Conduct a survey to determine how all organization involved in the JSWIM network collect, process, store, and quality assure salinity network information.

- Develop a plan that specifies which organizations will be responsible for each of the necessary quality-assurance measures.

- Develop SOPs designed for salinity sampling in existing network wells.

- Develop a network quality-assurance plan.

- Examine trends in water-level and salinity data to determine where changes are occurring.

- Evaluate and determine a schedule for desired network improvements.

- Evaluate and address known well condition or missing information issues.

- Develop a schedule to address well condition or missing information issues.

- Conduct a well inventory to identify any wells that could be added to fill gaps in the SFWMD-SWIMM network.

- Institute annual well depth checks and graphic evaluations of long-term data.

- Establish training to inform JSWIM personnel of quality assurance requirements and the SOPs designed for salinity sampling.

- Update aquifer assignments.

- Improve monitoring of canal salinity.

- Conduct borehole geophysical logging of wells with long open-borehole intervals.

- Drill test wells or collect surface geophysical measurements to determine the required locations for new monitoring wells.

- Collect geochemical samples to evaluate sources of saltwater.

- Install new wells to provide improved monitoring and delineation of saltwater intrusion.

- Collect detailed stratigraphic and geophysical data during well installation.

- Collect TSEMIL datasets from new wells.

- Abandon existing wells that no longer meet the needs of the network or that may allow saltwater intrusion between aquifers.

- Improve data dissemination.

- Determine a schedule for periodic reevaluations of the JSWIM network to track improvements and evaluate where changes are needed.

## Acknowledgments

The author would like to acknowledge the efforts of Anne Dodd, Kent Feng, Peter Kwiatkowski, and Herman Taub of the South Florida Water Management District, Ray Smith of the Collier County Pollution Control and Prevention Department, and Rick Copeland of the Florida Department of Environmental Protection for their substantive and insightful reviews of this report. Rhonda Watkins of Collier County Pollution Control and Prevention Department, Lee Werst of Lee County Natural Resources Division, and Cindy Bevier and Donna Rickabus of the South Florida Water Management District provided much of the data used in the evaluation of the salinity monitoring network in southwest Florida that is described in this report.

Kay Naugle, Eduardo Patino, and Chester Zenone of the U.S. Geological Survey provided substantive reviews of this report. Kim Swidarski of the U.S. Geological Survey created the final versions of the numerous figures provided in this report.

# Selected References

Abtew, Wossenu, Huebner R.S., and Sunderland, Simon, 2003, Hydrological analysis of the 2000–2001 drought in South Florida, Part I: South Florida Water Management District Drought Report, 98 p.

ASTM International, 1996a, Standard test method (analytical procedure) for determining transmissivity of nonleaky confined aquifers by overdamped well response to instantaneous change in head (slug tests): West Conshohocken, Pa., ASTM International, ASTM Standard D4104 – 96(2010)e1, 4 p. (Reapproved 2010; accessed April 11, 2012, at *http://dx.doi.org/10.1520/D4104-96R10E01.*)

ASTM International, 1996b, Standard test method for (field procedure) for instantaneous change in head (slug) tests for determining hydraulic properties of aquifers: West Conshohocken, Pa., ASTM International, ASTM Standard D4044 – 96(2008), 3 p. (Reapproved 2008; accessed April 11, 2012, at *http://dx.doi.org/10.1520/D4044-96.*)

ASTM International, 2001, Standard guide for conducting borehole geophysical logging—Electromagnetic induction: West Conshohocken, Pa., ASTM International, ASTM Standard D6726-01(2007), 8 p. (Reapproved 2007; accessed April 11, 2012, at *http://dx.doi.org/10.1520/D6726-01R07.*)

BEM Systems Inc., 2003, Hydrostratigraphy review report, Report to the Lower West Coast Regional Service Center: South Florida Water Management District, 40 p. (Available by request from the South Florida Water Management District.)

Boggess, D.H., Missimer T.M., and O'Donnell, T.H., 1977, Saline water intrusion related to well construction in Lee County, Florida: U.S. Geological Survey Water-Resources Investigations Report 77–33, 29 p.

Boggess, D.H., Missimer T.M., and O'Donnell, T.H., 1981, Hydrogeologic cross sections through Lee County and adjacent areas of Hendry and Collier Counties, Florida: U.S. Geological Survey Water-Resources Investigations Open-File Report 81–638, 1 sheet.

Burns, W.S., and Shih, George, 1984, Preliminary evaluation of the groundwater monitoring network in Collier County, Florida: Big Cypress Basin Board of the South Florida Water Management District, DRE 181, 46 p., 2 apps.

California Environmental Protection Agency, 1995, Aquifer testing for hydrogeologic characterization: Guidance manual for groundwater investigations: State of California Environmental Protection Agency, 26 p.

Campbell, K.M., 1988, The geology of Collier County, Florida: State of Florida Department of Natural Resources, Division of Resource Management, Florida Geological Survey, Open-File Report 25, 19 p.

Church, P.E., and Granato, G.E., 1996, Bias in ground-water data caused by well-bore flow in long screen wells: Ground Water, v. 34, no. 2, p. 262–273.

Cross, W.P., and Love, S.K., 1942, Groundwater in southeastern Florida: Journal of the American Water Works Association, v. 34, no. 4, p. 490–504.

Cunningham, K.J., Bukry, David, Sato, Tokiyuki, Barron, J.A., Guertin, L.A., and Reese, R.S., 2001a, Sequence stratigraphy of a south Florida carbonate ramp and bounding siliciclastics (late Miocene-Pliocene), *in* Missimer, T.M., and Scott, T.M., eds., Geology and hydrology of Lee County, Florida, Durward H. Boggess Memorial Symposium: Florida Geological Survey Special Publication No. 49, p. 35–66.

Cunningham, K.J., Locker, S.D., Hine, A.C., Bukry, David, Barron, J.A., and Guertin, L.A., 2001b, Surface-geophysical characterization of ground-water systems of the Caloosahatchee River Basin, Southern Florida: U.S. Geological Survey Water-Resources Investigations Report 01–4084, 36 p., 1 app.

Cunningham, K.J., Locker, S.D., Hine, A.C., Bukry, David, Barron, J.A., and Guertin L.A., 2003, Interplay of late Cenozoic siliciclastic supply and carbonate response on the southeast Florida Platform: Journal of Sedimentary Research, v. 73, no. 1, p. 31–46.

Cunningham, K.J., and Sukop, M.C., 2011, Multiple technologies applied to characterization of the porosity and permeability of the Biscayne aquifer, Florida: U.S. Geological Survey Open-File Report 2011–1037, 8 p., available at *http://pubs.usgs.gov/of/2011/1037.*

Cunningham, K.J., Sukop, M.C., Huang, H., Alvarez, P.F., Curran, H.A., Renken, R.A., and Dixon, J.F, 2009, Prominence of ichnologically influenced macroporosity in the karst Biscayne aquifer: Stratiform "super K" zones: Bulletin of the Geological Society of America, v. 121, no. 1/2, p. 164–180.

Cunningham, K.J., and Walker, C., 2009, Seismic-sag structural systems in tertiary carbonate rocks beneath southeastern Florida, U.S.A.: Evidence for hypogenic speleogeneis?: *in* Klimchouk, Alexander and Ford, Derek, eds., Hypogene speleogenesis and Karst hydrogeology of artesian basins: Ukrainian Institute of Speleology and Karstology, Special Paper 1, p. 151–158.

DuBar, J.R., 1991, Florida Peninsula, *in* DuBar, J.R., and others, Quaternary geology of the Gulf of Mexico coastal plain, chapter 19, *of* Morrison, R.B., ed., Quaternary nonglacial geology conterminous United States: Geological Society of America, The Geology of North America, The Decade of North American Geology (DNAG), v. K–2, p. 595–604.

Edwards, L.E., Weedman, S.D., Simmons, K.R., Scott, T.M., Brewster-Wingard, G.L., Ishman, S.E., and Carlin, N.M., 1998, Lithostratigraphy, peterology, biostratigraphy, and strontium-isotope stratigraphy of the surficial aquifer system of western Collier County, Florida: U.S. Geological Survey Open-File Report 98–205, 50 p., 2 app.

Fitterman, D.V., and Deszcz-Pan, M., 1998, Helicopter EM mapping of saltwater intrusion in Everglades National Park, Florida: Exploration Geophysics, v. 29, p. 240–243.

Fitterman, D.V. and Deszcz-Pan, M., 2002, Helicopter electromagnetic data from Everglades National Park and surrounding areas, Florida, collected 9–14 December 1994: U.S. Geological Survey Open-File Report 2002–101, 1 CD-ROM.

Fitterman, D.V., Deszcz-Pan, M., and Prinos, S.T., 2012, Helicopter electromagnetic survey of the Model Lands Area, southeastern Miami-Dade County, Florida: U.S. Geological Survey Open-File Report 2012–1176, 75 p., 1 app.

Fitterman, D.V., Deszcz-Pan, M., and Stoddard, C.E., 1999, Results of time-domain electromagnetic soundings in Everglades National Park, Florida: U.S. Geological Survey Open-File Report 99–426, 152 p. (CD-ROM)

Fitterman, D., and Prinos, S.T., 2011, Results of time-domain electromagnetic soundings in Miami-Dade and southern Broward Counties, Florida: U.S. Geological Survey Open-File Report 2011–1299, 42 p. appendixes, supplemental files download, accessed November 30, 2012, at *http://pubs.usgs.gov/of/2012/1176/downloads/*.

Fitzpatrick, D.J., 1986, Hydrogeologic conditions and saline-water intrusion, Cape Coral, Florida, 1978–81: U.S. Geological Survey Water-Resources Investigations Report 85–4231, 31 p.

Florida Department of Environmental Protection, 2008a, Monitoring well design and construction guidance manual: Florida Department of Environmental Protection Bureau of Water Facilities Regulation, 60 p., 3 apps.

Florida Department of Environmental Protection, 2008b, Groundwater sampling: Florida Department of Environmental Protection, Standard Operating Procedures, DEP-SOP-001/01 FS2200, 26 p., app.

Florida Department of Environmental Protection, 2012, Information about STORET: Florida Department of Environmental Protection, accessed April 30, 2012, at *http://survey.dep.state.fl.us/DearSpa/default.do?page=about*.

Florida Department of Health, 2005, Chemicals in private drinking water wells: Florida Department of Health, Fact sheet: Sodium, Florida Department of Health, 2 p.

Ghyben, W.B., 1889, Nota in verband met de voorgenomen put boring nabij Amsterdam; K. Inst Ing. Tijdschr, 1888–89: The Hague, p. 21.

Green, R.C., Campbell, K.M., and Scott, T.M., 1990, Core drilling project: Lee, Hendry and Collier Counties: Florida Geological Survey Open-File Report 37, 44 p.

Halford, K.J, Kuniansky, E.L., 2002, Documentation of spreadsheets for the analysis of aquifer-test and slug-test data: U.S. Geological Survey Open-File Report 02–197, 61 p.

Herzberg, A., 1901, Die Wasserversorgung einiger Nord-seebader [The water supply on parts of the North Sea coast]: Munich, Jour. Gasbeleuchtung und Wasser versorgung, v. 44, p. 815–819, 842–844.

Hittle, C.D., 1999, Delineation of saltwater intrusion in the surficial aquifer system, in eastern Palm Beach, Martin, and St. Lucie Counties, Florida, 1997–98: U.S. Geological Survey Water-Resources Investigations Report 99–4214, 1 sheet.

Hunter, M.E., 1968, Molluscan guide fossils in late Miocene sediments of southern Florida: Gulf Coast Association of Geological Societies Transactions, v. 18, p. 439–450.

Indiana Department of Environmental Management, 1998, The mirco-purge sampling option: Indiana Department of Environmental Management, Technical guidance document, revised 2009, 6 p., accessed May 17, 2012, at *http://www.in.gov/idem/files/remediation_tech_guidance_micro-purge.pdf*.

Intergovernmental Panel on Climate Change (IPCC), 2007, Climate change 2007: Synthesis report: Contribution of Working Groups I, II and III to the Fourth Assessment Report of the Intergovernmental Panel on Climate Change [Core writing team, Pachauri, R.K., and Reisinger, A., eds.]: IPCC, Geneva, Switzerland, 104 p.

Jakob , P.G., 1983, Hydrogeology of the shallow aquifer south of Naples, Collier County: South Florida Water Management District, Technical Publication No. 83–3, 52 p., 3 apps., 11 pages of logs.

Johnson, C.D., Haeni, F.P., Lane, J.W., and White, E.A., 2002, Borehole-geophysical examination of the University of Connecticut landfill, Storrs, Connecticut: U.S. Geological Survey Water-Resources Investigations Report 01–4033, 42 p.

Kalford, K.J., and Kuniansky, E.L., 2002, Documentation of spreadsheets for the analysis of aquifer-test and slug-test data: U.S. Geological Survey Open-File Report 02–197, 51 p., accessed May 9, 2012, at *http://pubs.usgs.gov/ of/2002/ofr02197/*.

Kearl, P.M., Korte, N.E., Stites, Mike, and Baker, Joe, 1994, Field comparison of micropurging vs. traditional groundwater sampling: National Ground Water Association, Ground Water Monitoring & Remediation, v. 14, no. 4, p. 183–190.

Klein, Howard, 1954, Ground-water resources of the Naples area, Collier County, Florida: Florida Geological Survey Report of Investigations No. 11, 64 p.

Klein, Howard, 1980, Water-resources investigations, Collier County, Florida: U.S. Geological Survey Open-File Report 80–1270, 29 p.

Knapp, M.S., Burns, W.S., and Sharp, T.S., 1986, Preliminary assessment of the groundwater resources of western Collier County, Florida: South Florida Water Management District, Technical Publication 86–1, Part 1, 142 p.

Kohout, F.A., 1964, The flow of fresh water and salt water in the Biscayne aquifer of the Miami area, Florida, *in* Cooper, H.H., Jr., Kohout, F.A., Henry, H.R., and Glover, R.E., Sea water in coastal aquifers: U.S. Geological Survey Water-Supply Paper 1613–C, p. C12–C32.

Kohout, F.A., and Hoy, N.D., 1963, Some aspects of sampling salty ground water in coastal aquifers: Ground Water, v. 1, no. 1, p. 28–32.

Kohout, F.A., and Leach, S.D., 1964, Saltwater movement caused by control-dam operation in the Snake Creek Canal, Miami Florida, State of Florda, State Board of Conservation, Division of Geology, Florida Geological Survey, Report of Investigations, no. 24, part IV, 49 p.

Lane, S.L., Flanagan, Sarah, and Wilde, F.D., 2003, Selection of equipment for water sampling (ver. 2.0): U.S. Geological Survey Techniques of Water-Resources Investigations, book 9, chap. A2, March 2003, accessed November 15, 2012, at *http://pubs.water.usgs.gov/twri9A2/*.

Lapham, W.W., Wilde, F.D., and Koterba, M.T., 1997, Guidelines and standard procedures for studies of ground-water quality: Selection and installation of wells, and supporting documentation: U.S. Geological Survey Water-Resources Investigations Report 96–4233, 110 p.

La Rose, H.R., 1990, Geohydrologic framework and an analysis of a well-plugging program, Lee County, Florida: U.S. Geological Survey Water-Resources Investigations Report 90–4063, 26 p.

Leach S.D., and Grantham R.G., 1966, Salt-water study of the Miami River and its tributaries, Dade County, Florida: Florida Geological Survey Report of Investigations No. 45, 35 p.

Lee County Natural Resources Division, 2012, Surface Water Monitoring System: Lee County Natural Resources Division, accessed May 2, 2012, at *http://leegis.leegov.com/ surfacewater/*.

Marella, R.L., 2009, Water withdrawals, use, and trends in Florida, 2005: U.S. Geological Survey Scientific Investigations Report 2009–5125, p.11.

Matson, G.C., and Sanford, Samuel, 1913, Geology and ground waters of Florida: U.S. Geological Survey Water-Supply Paper 319, 445 p.

McCoy, H.J., 1962, Ground-water resources of Collier County, Florida: Florida Geological Survey Report of Investigations No. 31, 82 p.

McCoy Jack, 1972, Hydrology of western Collier County, Florida: State of Florida Department of Natural Resources, Report of Investigations No. 63, 32 p.

McIlvride, W.A., and Rector, B.M., 1988, Comparison of short- and long-screen monitoring wells in alluvial sediments, *in* Proceedings of the Second National Outdoor Action Conference on Aquifer Restoration, Ground Water Monitoring and Geophysical Methods, v. 1, May 23–26, 1988: Las Vegas, Nev., Ground Water Scientists and Engineers Association, p. 375–390.

McNeill, J.D., 1990, Use of electromagnetic methods for groundwater studies, *in* Ward, S.H., ed., Geotechnical and environmental geophysics: Tulsa, Society of Exploration Geophysicists, p. 191–218.

McNeil, J.D., Dosnar, M., and Snelgrove, F.B., 1990, Resolution of an electromagnetic borehole conductivity logger for geotechnical and ground water applications Mississauga, Ontario: Geonics Limited, Technical Note 25, 28 p.

McPherson, B.F., and Halley, Robert, 1996, The South Florida Environment: A region under stress: U.S. Geological Survey Circular 1134, 61 p.

Missimer, T.M., 1993, Pliocene stratigraphy of south Florida: Unresolved issues of facies correlation in time, *in* Zullo, V.A., Harris, W.B., Scott, T.M., and Portell, R.W., eds., The Neogene of Florida and adjacent regions: Proceedings of the Third Bald Head Island Conference on Coastal Plains Geology: Florida Geological Survey Special Publication 37, p. 33–42.

Missimer, T.M., 1997, Late Paleogene and Neogene sea level history of the southern Florida platform based on seismic and sequence stratigraphy: Miami, University of Miami, Ph.D. dissertation, 942 p.

Missimer, T.M., 2001, Late Neogene Geology of northwestern Lee County, Florida, in Geology and hydrology of Lee County, Florida, Durwood H. Boggess Memorial Symposium: Florida Geological Survey Special Publication No. 49, 231 p.

Missimer, T.M., and Scott, T.M., eds., 2001, Geology and hydrology of Lee County, Florida, Durwood H. Boggess Memorial Symposium: Florida Geological Survey Special Publication No. 49, 231 p.

National Oceanic and Atmospheric Administration, 2012, Sea levels online: National Oceanic and Atmospheric Administration, accessed November 30, 2012, at *http:// tidesandcurrents.noaa.gov/sltrends/sltrends.shtml*.

New Mexico Environment Department Waste Bureau, 2001, Use of low-flow and other non-traditional sampling techniques for RCRA compliant groundwater monitoring: Hazardous Waste Bureau, New Mexico Environment Department, Position Paper, 15 p., accessed November 14, 2012, at *http://www.nmenv.state.nm.us/HWB/ data/11-7low-flow_final.pdf*.

Oki, D.S., and Presley T.K., 2008, Causes of borehole flow and effects on vertical salinity profiles in coastal aquifers: Program and proceedings book, 20th Salt Water Intrusion Meeting, June 23–27, 2008, p. 170–173, accessed November 14, 2012, at *http://conference.ifas.ufl.edu/swim/ papers.pdf*.

Parker, G.G., 1945, Salt water encroachment in southern Florida: Journal of the American Water Works Association, v. 37, no. 6, p. 526–542.

Parker, G.G., Ferguson, G.E., Love, S.K., and others, 1955, Water resources of southeastern Florida, with special reference to the geology and ground water of the Miami area: U.S. Geological Survey Water-Supply Paper 1255, 965 p.

Peacock, R.S., 1983, The post-Eocene stratigraphy of southern Collier County, Florida: South Florida Water Management District, Technical Publication 83–5, 42 p, 4 apps.

Peck, D.M, Slater, D.H., Missimer, T.M., Wise, S.W., Jr., and O'Donnell, T.H., 1979, Stratigraphy and paleoecology of the Tamiami Formation in Lee and Hendry Counties, Florida: Gulf Coast Association of Geological Societies, Transactions, v. 39, p. 328–341.

Prinos, S.T., Lietz, A.C., and Irvin, R.B., 2002, Design of a real-time ground-water level monitoring network and portrayal of hydrologic data in southern Florida: U.S. Geological Survey Water-Resources Investigations Report 01–4275, 108 p.

Reese, R.S., 2000, Hydrogeology and the distribution of salinity in the Floridan aquifer system, southwestern Florida: U.S. Geological Survey Water-Resources Investigations Report 98–4253, 59 p., 3 apps.

Reese, R.S., and Cunningham, K.J., 2000, Hydrogeology of the gray limestone aquifer in southern Florida: U.S. Geological Survey Water-Resources Investigations Report 99–4213, 244 p.

Reilly, T.E., Franke, O.L., and Bennett, G.D., 1989, Bias in groundwater samples caused by wellbore flow: Hydraulic Engineering Journal, v. 115, no. 2, p. 270–276.

Renken, R.A., Cunningham, K.J., Shapiro, A.M., Harvey, R.W., Zygnerski, M.R., Metge, D.W., and Wacker, M.A., 2008, Pathogen and chemical transport in the karst limestone of the Biscayne aquifer: 1. Revised conceptualization of groundwater flow, Water Resources Research 44, W08429, doi:10.1029/2007WR006058.

Richter, B.C., and Kreitler, C.W., 1993, Geochemical techniques for identifying sources of ground-water salinization: CRC Press, Boca Raton, Fla., 258 p.

Runkel, A.C., Tipping, R.G., and Anderson, J.R., 2008, Washington County landfill logging project: Borehole geophysical tests for presences of fracture flow at a perflourochemical contamination site: Minnesota Geological Survey, Open-File Report 08–07, 9 p. plus figs. and 1 app.

Schlosser, Peter, Stute, Martin, Dörr, Helmut, Sonntag, Christian, and Munnich, K.O., 1988, Tritium/3He dating of shallow groundwater: Earth and Planetary Science Letters, v. 89, p. 353–362

Schlumberger Water Services USA Inc., 2010, Big Cypress Basin Saltwater Intrusion Pilot Modeling Study, Phase II, Schlumberger Water Services USA Inc. Project Number 0092–163, 23 p., apps.

Schmerge, D.L., 2001, Distribution and origin of salinity in the surficial and intermediate aquifer systems, southwestern Florida: U.S. Geological Survey Water-Resources Investigations Report 2001–4159, 41 p.

Shalev, E., Lazar, A., Wollam, S., Kington, S., Yechieli, Y., and Gvirtzman, H., 2009, Biased monitoring of fresh water-salt water mixing zone in coastal aquifers: Ground Water, v. 47, no. 1, p. 49–56.

Shapiro, A.M., 2002, Cautions and suggestions for geochemical sampling in fractured rock: Groundwater Monitoring & Remediation 22, no. 3, p. 151–164.

Sherwood, C.B., and Klein, Howard, 1961, Groundwater resources of northwestern Collier County, Florida: Florida Geological Survey, Information Circular No. 29, 44 p.

Sherwood, C.B., and Klein, Howard, 1962, Saline ground-water in southern Florida: Proceedings from the National Water Well Exposition, October 1962: National Water Well Association, p. 4–8.

Shoemaker, B.W., and Edwards, K.M., 2003, Potential for saltwater intrusion into the lower Tamiami aquifer near Bonita Springs: U.S. Geological Survey Water-Resources Investigations Report 03–4262, 66 p., 1 app.

Smith, K.R., and Adams, K.M., 1988, Ground water assessment of Hendry County, Florida: South Florida Water Management District Technical Publication 88–12, 109 p.

Sonenshein, R.S., 1997, Delineation and extent of saltwater intrusion in the Biscayne aquifer, eastern Dade County, Florida 1995: U.S. Geological Survey Water-Resources Investigations Report 96–4285, 1 sheet.

South Florida Water Management District, 2006, Quick facts on Golden Gate canal improvements: managing a limited system in a high growth area: South Florida Water Management, accessed June 13, 2011, at *http://www.sfwmd.gov/portal/page/portal/pg_grp_sfwmd_regionalserv/portlet_bcbprojects/golden_gate_canal.pdf.*

South Florida Water Management District, 2009, Climate change & water management in south Florida, Interdepartmental Climate Change Group: South Florida Water Management District, White Paper, 20 p.

South Florida Water Management District, 2010, Big Cypress Basin strategic plan: 2010 ~2015: South Florida Water Management, 12 p., accessed June 1, 2012, at *http://my.sfwmd.gov/portal/page/portal/xrepository/sfwmd_repository_pdf/2010_strategic%20plan_bcb.pdf.*

South Florida Water Management District, 2011a, Collier County, estimated position of the saltwater interface, surficial/water table aquifer: South Florida Water Management, 1 sheet.

South Florida Water Management District, 2011b, Lee and Collier counties, estimated position of the saltwater interface, lower Tamiami aquifer: South Florida Water Management, 1 sheet.

South Florida Water Management District, 2012, DBHYDRO (Environmental Data): South Florida Water Management District, accessed May 2, 2012, at *http://www.sfwmd.gov/portal/page/portal/xweb%20environmental %20monitoring/dbhydro%20application.*

Southeastern Geological Society Ad Hoc Committee on Florida Hydrostratigraphic Unit Definition, 1986, Hydrogeologic units of Florida: Florida Geological Survey Special Publication No. 28, 9 p.

Stewart, M.A. Bhatt, T.N., Fennema, R.J., and Fitterman, D.V., 2002, The road to flamingo: An evaluation of flow pattern alterations and salinity intrusion in the lower glades, Everglades National Park: U.S. Geological Survey Open-File Report 2002–59, 36 p.

Swayze, L.J., and McPherson, B.F., 1977, The effect of the FAKA Union Canal System on water levels in the Fakahatchee Strand, Collier County, Florida: U.S. Geological Survey, Water-Resources Investigations Report 77–61, 19 p.

U.S. Army Corps of Engineers, and the South Florida Water Management District, 2004, Comprehensive Everglades restoration plan: Picayune Strand restoration final integrated project implementation report and environmental impact statement: U.S. Army Corps of Engineers, and the South Florida Water Management District, accessed October 2, 2012, at *http://www.evergladesplan.org/pm/projects/docs_30_sgge_pir_final.aspx.*

U.S. Census Bureau, 2011, Population estimates, counties: U.S. Census Bureau, accessed June 8, 2011, at *http://www.census.gov/popest/counties/.*

U.S. Environmental Protection Agency, 1991, Handbook of suggested practices for the design and installation of ground-water monitoring wells: U.S. Environmental Protection Agency, EPA/600/4-89/034, 139 p., 2 apps.

U.S. Environmental Protection Agency, 2011a, Secondary drinking water regulations; guidance for nuisance chemicals: U.S. Environmental Protection Agency, 816-f-10-079, accessed January 26, 2011, at *http://water.epa.gov/drink/contaminants/secondarystandards.cfm.*

U.S. Environmental Protection Agency, 2011b, Drinking water contaminants: National primary drinking water standards: U.S. Environmental Protection Agency, accessed February 23, 2011, at *http://water.epa.gov/drink/contaminants/index.cfm.*

U.S. Geological Survey, 2012a, Current water-level conditions in south Florida: U.S. Geological Survey accessed June 1, 2012, at *http://www.sflorida.er.usgs.gov/ddn_data/index_ndt.html.*

U.S. Geological Survey, 2012b, USGS water data for the Nation: U.S. Geological Survey, accessed June 1, 2012, at *http://waterdata.usgs.gov/nwis.*

U.S. Geological Survey, 2012c, Groundwater conditions in southern Florida: U.S. Geological Survey, accessed June 1, 2012, at *http://www.sflorida.er.usgs.gov/edl_data/index_ndt.html.*

U.S. Geological Survey, 2012d, Saline intrusion monitoring, Miami-Dade County, Florida: U.S. Geological Survey, accessed June 1, 2012, at *http://www.envirobase.usgs.gov/ FLIMS/SaltFront/viewer.htm*.

U.S. Geological Survey, 2012e, Water resources groundwater software: U.S. Geological Survey, accessed June 1, 2012, at *http://water.usgs.gov/software/lists/groundwater*.

U.S. Geological Survey, 2012f, National Geologic Map Database: Geolex database: U.S. Geological Survey, accessed September 10, 2012, at *http://ngmdb.usgs.gov/Geolex/*.

U.S. Geological Survey, variously dated, National field manual for the collection of water-quality data: U.S. Geological Survey Techniques of Water-Resources Investigations, book 9, chaps. A1–A9, accessed March 27, 2013, *http:// pubs.water.usgs.gov/twri9A*.

Verdi, R.J., Tomlinson, S.A., and Marella, R.L., 2006, The drought of 1998–2002: Impacts on Florida's hydrology and landscape: U.S. Geological Survey Circular 1295, 34 p.

Wacker, M.A., and Cunningham, K.J., 2008, Borehole geophysical logging program: Incorporating new and existing techniques in hydrologic studies: U.S. Geological Survey Fact Sheet 2008–3098, 4 p.

Wedderburn, L.A., Knapp, M.S., Waltz, D.P., and Burns, W.S., 1982, Hydrogeologic reconnaissance of Lee County, Florida: South Florida Water Management District, Technical Publication 82–1, 192 p.

www.ingramcontent.com/pod-product-compliance
Lightning Source LLC
Chambersburg PA
CBHW080437290526
45791CB00008BA/2537